Improving Consent and Response in Longitudinal Studies of Aging

PROCEEDINGS OF A WORKSHOP

Brian Harris-Kojetin, *Rapporteur*

Improving Consent and Response in Longitudinal Studies of Aging:
A Workshop

Committee on National Statistics

Division of Behavioral and Social Sciences and Education

The National Academies of
SCIENCES • ENGINEERING • MEDICINE

THE NATIONAL ACADEMIES PRESS
Washington, DC
www.nap.edu

THE NATIONAL ACADEMIES PRESS   500 Fifth Street, NW   Washington, DC 20001

This activity was supported by a contract between the National Academy of Sciences and the U.S. Department of Health and Human Services (award HHSN263201800029I/75N98020F00026). Any opinions, findings, conclusions, or recommendations expressed in this publication do not necessarily reflect the views of any organization or agency that provided support for the project.

International Standard Book Number-13: 978-0-309-28670-1
International Standard Book Number-10: 0-309-28670-0
Digital Object Identifier: https://doi.org/10.17226/26481

This publication is available from the National Academies Press, 500 Fifth Street, NW, Keck 360, Washington, DC 20001; (800) 624-6242 or (202) 334-3313; http://www.nap.edu.

Copyright 2022 by the National Academy of Sciences. All rights reserved.

Printed in the United States of America

Suggested citation: National Academies of Sciences, Engineering, and Medicine. 2022. *Improving Consent and Response in Longitudinal Studies of Aging: Proceedings of a Workshop*. Washington, DC: The National Academies Press. https://doi.org/10.17226/26481.

The National Academies of
SCIENCES · ENGINEERING · MEDICINE

The **National Academy of Sciences** was established in 1863 by an Act of Congress, signed by President Lincoln, as a private, nongovernmental institution to advise the nation on issues related to science and technology. Members are elected by their peers for outstanding contributions to research. Dr. Marcia McNutt is president.

The **National Academy of Engineering** was established in 1964 under the charter of the National Academy of Sciences to bring the practices of engineering to advising the nation. Members are elected by their peers for extraordinary contributions to engineering. Dr. John L. Anderson is president.

The **National Academy of Medicine** (formerly the Institute of Medicine) was established in 1970 under the charter of the National Academy of Sciences to advise the nation on medical and health issues. Members are elected by their peers for distinguished contributions to medicine and health. Dr. Victor J. Dzau is president.

The three Academies work together as the **National Academies of Sciences, Engineering, and Medicine** to provide independent, objective analysis and advice to the nation and conduct other activities to solve complex problems and inform public policy decisions. The National Academies also encourage education and research, recognize outstanding contributions to knowledge, and increase public understanding in matters of science, engineering, and medicine.

Learn more about the National Academies of Sciences, Engineering, and Medicine at **www.nationalacademies.org**.

The National Academies of
SCIENCES · ENGINEERING · MEDICINE

Consensus Study Reports published by the National Academies of Sciences, Engineering, and Medicine document the evidence-based consensus on the study's statement of task by an authoring committee of experts. Reports typically include findings, conclusions, and recommendations based on information gathered by the committee and the committee's deliberations. Each report has been subjected to a rigorous and independent peer-review process and it represents the position of the National Academies on the statement of task.

Proceedings published by the National Academies of Sciences, Engineering, and Medicine chronicle the presentations and discussions at a workshop, symposium, or other event convened by the National Academies. The statements and opinions contained in proceedings are those of the participants and are not endorsed by other participants, the planning committee, or the National Academies.

Rapid Expert Consultations published by the National Academies of Sciences, Engineering, and Medicine are authored by subject-matter experts on narrowly focused topics that can be supported by a body of evidence. The discussions contained in rapid expert consultations are considered those of the authors and do not contain policy recommendations. Rapid expert consultations are reviewed by the institution before release.

For information about other products and activities of the National Academies, please visit www.nationalacademies.org/about/whatwedo.

PLANNING COMMITTEE ON IMPROVING CONSENT AND RESPONSE IN LONGITUDINAL STUDIES OF AGING

MICHAEL DAVERN (*Chair*), Executive Vice President, NORC at the University of Chicago
MICK P. COUPER, Research Professor, University of Michigan
JENNIFER MADANS, retired, National Center for Health Statistics
SUNITA SAH, Associate Professor, University of Cambridge and Cornell University
VETTA SANDERS THOMPSON, Professor, Washington University in St. Louis

Study Staff

BRIAN HARRIS-KOJETIN, *Study Director*
REBECCA KRONE, *Program Coordinator*

COMMITTEE ON NATIONAL STATISTICS

ROBERT M. GROVES (*Chair*), Office of the Provost, Georgetown University
LAWRENCE D. BOBO, Department of Sociology, Harvard University
ANNE C. CASE, Princeton School of Public and International Affairs, Princeton University, *Emeritus*
MICK P. COUPER, Institute for Social Research, University of Michigan
JANET M. CURRIE, Princeton School of Public and International Affairs, Princeton University
DIANA FARRELL, JPMorgan Chase Institute, Washington, DC
ROBERT GOERGE, Chapin Hall at the University of Chicago
ERICA L. GROSHEN, School of Industrial and Labor Relations, Cornell University
HILARY HOYNES, Goldman School of Public Policy, University of California-Berkeley
DANIEL KIFER, Department of Computer Science and Engineering, The Pennsylvania State University
SHARON LOHR, School of Mathematical and Statistical Sciences, Arizona State University, *Emeritus*
JEROME P. REITER, Department of Statistical Science, Duke University
JUDITH A. SELTZER, Department of Sociology, University of California-Los Angeles, *Emeritus*
C. MATTHEW SNIPP, School of the Humanities and Sciences, Stanford University
ELIZABETH A. STUART, Department of Mental Health, Johns Hopkins Bloomberg School of Public Health
JEANNETTE WING, Data Science Institute and Computer Science Department, Columbia University

Staff

BRIAN HARRIS-KOJETIN, *Director*
MELISSA CHIU, *Deputy Director*
CONSTANCE F. CITRO, *Senior Scholar*

Acknowledgments

This Proceedings of a Workshop was reviewed in draft form by individuals chosen for their diverse perspectives and technical expertise. The purpose of this independent review is to provide candid and critical comments that will assist the National Academies of Sciences, Engineering, and Medicine in making each published proceedings as sound as possible and to ensure that it meets the institutional standards for quality, objectivity, evidence, and responsiveness to the charge. The review comments and draft manuscript remain confidential to protect the integrity of the process.

We thank **MICK P. COUPER**, Institute for Social Research, University of Michigan, for his review of this proceedings. We also thank staff member Sheena Posey Norris for reading and providing helpful comments on this manuscript.

Although the reviewers listed above provided many constructive comments and suggestions, they were not asked to endorse the conclusions or recommendations of this report nor did they see the final draft before its release. The review of this report was overseen by **JUDITH SELTZER**, Department of Sociology, University of California-Los Angeles, Emeritus. She was responsible for making certain that an independent examination of this report was carried out in accordance with the standards of the National Academies and that all review comments were carefully considered. Responsibility for the final content rests entirely with the authoring committee and the National Academies.

Contents

1 Introduction — 1
THE NATIONAL INSTITUTE ON AGING'S PERSPECTIVE ON KEY ISSUES FOR THE WORKSHOP TO ADDRESS, 2
THE PLANNING COMMITTEE'S GOALS FOR THE WORKSHOP, 3
ORGANIZATION OF THE REPORT, 4

2 Background and Context — 7
OPPORTUNITIES AND CHALLENGES WITH RESPONSE AND CONSENT IN LONGITUDINAL SURVEYS ON AGING, 7
IDENTIFYING AND REDUCING SELECTION BIAS, 20

3 Participation — 31
MAXIMIZING RESPONDENT RETENTION, 31
PARTICIPANT ENGAGEMENT: INSIGHTS FROM BEHAVIORAL SCIENCE RESEARCH, 41

4 Informed Consent — 49
THE COMPLEXITY OF INFORMED CONSENT, 49
ETHICAL CONSIDERATIONS FOR OBTAINING INFORMED CONSENT, 58

5 Data Linkage and Innovation 71
DATA LINKAGE, 71
LOOKING AHEAD: APPLYING INNOVATIVE STRATEGIES
  TO IMPROVE CONSENT AND RESPONSE, 79

6 Wrap-Up Discussion 93
TAKE-HOME POINTS AND RESEARCH PRIORITIES, 93
DISCUSSION OF ADDITIONAL PRIORITIES FOR FUTURE
  RESEARCH, 97
NIA PERSPECTIVES ON THE WORKSHOP, 99

References 101

Appendix A Public Meeting Agenda 103
Appendix B Committee and Speaker Biosketches 107

Box, Figures, and Tables

BOX

1-1 Statement of Task, 3

FIGURES

2-1 Core interview response rates for the Health and Retirement Study, 1994–2020, 17
2-2 Cumulative responses by wave and effort (cumulative number of call attempts), 18

3-1 Proportion of previous wave respondents who were re-interviewed at each wave shown separately by age group, 32

4-1 How respondents decide whether to consent, 51
4-2 NSHAP BioBox for remote collection in Round 4, 55

5-1 Availability of survey and Medicare data, 73
5-2 Model respondent's decision whether to participate in additional tasks, 82
5-3 The American Opportunity Study backbone and opportunities for survey linkages, 86
5-4 Average absolute bias for variables from a past round and from the sampling frame from the 2013 Update of the High School Longitudinal Study of 2009, 89

TABLES

2-1 MIDUS Response Rates, 8
2-2 Add Health Longitudinal Design, 13
2-3 Add Health Wave 5 Response and Consent Rates, 14
2-4 CATI/CAPI Cross-Sectional Survey of Welfare Benefit Recipients in Germany (administrative records available for drawn sample), 21
2-5 Adjusting for Panel Nonresponse Bias Using Previous Wave(s) Survey Data, 22
2-6 Treatments Used in 2016/2017 Baccalaureate and Beyond Longitudinal Study (B&B) Field Test, 27
2-7 Results from 2016/2017 Baccalaureate and Beyond Longitudinal Study (B&B) Field Test, 27

3-1 Results of Different Data Collection Procedures and Events on Re-engaging Nonrespondents and Continuing Participation of Respondents, 33

4-1 NSHAP In-Person Biomeasure Cooperation Rates, 54

1

Introduction

This Proceedings of a Workshop summarizes the presentations and discussions at the Workshop on Improving Consent and Response in Longitudinal Studies of Aging, which was held virtually and live-streamed on September 27–28, 2021. The workshop was convened by the Committee on National Statistics (CNSTAT) of the National Academies of Science, Engineering, and Medicine to assist the National Institute on Aging (NIA) with its methodological research agenda and inform the different longitudinal survey programs sponsored by NIA about practices and research to improve response and consent in other survey programs.

The workshop was structured to bring together scientists and researchers from multiple disciplines and countries to share their research and insights on how to improve response and consent in large, representative longitudinal studies on aging. The workshop agenda is provided in Appendix A. Biographical sketches of the steering committee members and workshop presenters are included in Appendix B.

The mission of CNSTAT is to provide advice to the federal government and the nation grounded in the current best scientific knowledge and practice that will lead to improved statistical methods and information upon which to base public policy. CNSTAT seeks to advance the quality of statistical information, contribute to the statistical policies and coordinating activities of the federal government, and help provide a forward-looking vision for the federal statistical system and national statistics more broadly in service of the public good. In introductory remarks, CNSTAT's director, Brian Harris-Kojetin, thanked NIA for the opportunity to convene this workshop.

THE NATIONAL INSTITUTE ON AGING'S PERSPECTIVE ON KEY ISSUES FOR THE WORKSHOP TO ADDRESS

John Phillips, chief of the Population and Social Processes Branch (PSP) of the NIA Division of Behavioral and Social Research (BSR), introduced the reason behind the workshop by underscoring that survey response and retention rates are declining across longitudinal and cross-sectional studies around the world. Given the importance of this subject to so many research enterprises, a body of published research has emerged on protocols intended to explore these issues. However, he said, much of this research focuses on cross-sectional surveys or is not directed toward midlife or older populations or rare populations of interest for studies of health disparities. He suggested greater understanding of the factors that limit consent and response in surveys could lead to better ways to inform participants about the benefits of study participation and risks of consent, as well as provide significant value to both aging studies and to the survey research literature.

NIA supports several nationally representative longitudinal studies, each with unique structural features to facilitate research on various dimensions of health and aging. NIA-supported longitudinal studies collect data covering many domains, including socioeconomic factors, self-reported and objective measures of health, cognition, personality, family structure, health care utilization and care needs, and even genetics. Some of these studies also include collection of blood samples or saliva, which typically require separate consent than the survey itself.

In addition, Phillips noted that the longitudinal studies that NIA supports often seek to link the survey data with federal program data, such as Social Security Administration records on earnings, and these linkages require separate consent. Combining survey, biological, and administrative data together provides a much more complete picture of life course health and aging, with objective measurement of important domains, and in some instances, less burden on respondents to provide information. However, increasing the number of questions asked, requesting biological samples, and asking permission to link to other government records can lead some respondents to reject one or more of those protocols or the study entirely, threatening the representativeness of the sample and quality of the data obtained.

Phillips summarized some recommendations from the 2019 National Advisory Council on Aging (NACA) review of BSR's extramural program related to response and consent rates in NIA-supported nationally representative longitudinal studies of aging. The top NACA recommendation was to focus on investigations of various disparities in health at older ages, which requires diverse representative national samples with high response and consent rates to limit the risk of nonresponse bias. The NACA recommendations also explicitly encouraged the continued collection and linkage of biology and program administrative data to NIA-supported studies, and recommended prioritizing research to develop new and more efficient methods for recruiting and retaining study participants to ensure samples are population representative.

Phillips concluded by saying that NIH has partnered with CNSTAT to convene the workshop to obtain expert opinion on how to improve response/retention and enhance consent protocols for biomarker and administrative data linkage in nationally representative longitudinal studies of older Americans to support innovative behavioral and social research on aging.

THE PLANNING COMMITTEE'S GOALS FOR THE WORKSHOP

The purpose of the workshop was "to discuss methods to improve response/retention and enhance consent protocols for biomarker and program (administrative) data linkage in nationally representative longitudinal studies of older Americans," according to the statement of task (Box 1-1). Michael Davern, chair of the planning committee and senior vice president and director of the Public Health Research Department at NORC at the University of Chicago, described the plan and goals for the workshop. First, he said, workshop sessions would examine innovations in survey methods with a multidisciplinary approach, such as framing of questions and consent

---

BOX 1-1
Statement of Task

An ad hoc planning committee of the National Academies of Sciences, Engineering, and Medicine will plan and execute a two-day public workshop to discuss methods to improve response/retention and enhance consent protocols for biomarker and program (administrative) data linkage in nationally representative longitudinal studies of older Americans. The methods discussed will include (1) innovations in survey methods with a multidisciplinary approach such as framing of questions and consent protocols employing insights from psychology and behavioral economics; (2) messaging and participant engagement approaches about the value of study participation; and (3) efforts to understand what would motivate consent to specific protocol and efforts to understand if a study has adequately secured a social license/trust with respondents.

The planning committee will define the specific topics to be addressed, develop the agenda, and invite speakers and other participants. After the workshop, proceedings of the workshop will be prepared by a designated rapporteur in accordance with institutional guidelines.

protocols employing insights from psychology, behavioral economics, and other disciplines. Second, the workshop would examine messaging and participant engagement approaches to make sure learning from the best and newest approaches is being used to engage and keep respondents engaged in longitudinal studies. Third, sessions would discuss efforts to understand what would motivate consent for administrative record linkage and consent to specific biomarker and physical measure protocols and procedures. Davern noted that all three goals are essential to what survey researchers who are engaged in studying the science of aging need to do.

As Davern described, surveys are currently at a moment of crisis, but this is certainly not the first crisis in survey research. There have been many changes in methodologies and approaches through the years, including integrating cell phones with landline phone surveys, and then dealing with the loss of landlines. He said that researchers have dealt with falling participation rates across all survey modes and with increasing costs of data collection. Concurring with Phillips, Davern noted the recent concerns are nonresponse bias and representativeness of surveys.

For Davern, the key question is how to adapt and change as a result of this crisis. This, he stressed, is the challenge that the industry needs to address because staying the course and doing what has always been done is not a good idea. He noted that the speakers during the workshop would provide insight into this question and help illuminate strategies to adapt, change, and resolve this current crisis.

ORGANIZATION OF THE REPORT

This summary describes the workshop presentations and discussions that followed each topic.[1] The chapters are organized around the sessions of the workshop, which included overviews of NIA-sponsored studies, participation, informed consent, and data linkage. The final sessions of the workshop focused on innovation and a wrap-up discussion in which Phillips and committee members pulled out what they saw as key themes and messages from across the workshop to help NIA move the work in this area forward.

The full meeting agenda and biographical sketches of steering committee members and workshop presenters appear in the appendixes. This proceedings has been prepared by the workshop rapporteur as a factual summary of what occurred at the workshop. The planning committee's role was limited to planning and convening the workshop. The views contained

---

[1] Presenters' slides and videos of the entire workshop are available at https://www.nationalacademies.org/event/09-27-2021/improving-consent-and-response-in-longitudinal-studies-of-aging-a-workshop.

in the proceedings are those of individual workshop participants and do not necessarily represent the views of all workshop participants, the planning committee, the National Institute on Aging, or the National Academies of Sciences, Engineering, and Medicine.

2

Background and Context

This chapter summarizes the presentations and discussion in the first two sessions of the workshop that provided an overview of four major NIA-sponsored studies by their principal investigators and presentations from three researchers on identifying and reducing nonresponse bias. Vetta Sanders Thompson from Washington University in St. Louis chaired the first session, and Jennifer Madans, formerly of the National Center for Health Statistics, chaired the second session.

OPPORTUNITIES AND CHALLENGES WITH RESPONSE AND CONSENT IN LONGITUDINAL SURVEYS ON AGING

Midlife in the United States (MIDUS)

Carol Ryff, the director of the Institute on Aging and Hilldale Professor of Psychology at the University of Wisconsin-Madison and principal investigator for MIDUS,[1] described what she and her colleagues have done in the MIDUS study to maximize participation. They have used incentives and sent newsletters and birthday cards to give back and build rapport with their respondents. MIDUS includes a nationally representative sample of over 11,000 Americans, all of whom were aged 25 to 74 at their baseline assessments. The study began in 1995 with over 7,000 adults, including a national sample of twins, all of whom completed a survey; a subsample also completed daily assessments.

---

[1] For more information, see http://www.midus.wisc.edu/index.php.

NIA began funding the project at the second wave, which collected the survey and daily assessments, but also added new projects on cognition, biomarkers, and neuroscience in 2004. Only the survey was attempted with all participants; the other assessments were only conducted on subsamples given the time and cost of these projects. Ryff noted that in 2012, they recruited a new national sample known as the Refresher that brought over 4,000 new participants to the study, paralleling the age and gender profiles of the core baseline sample. The same multiproject assessments were obtained on the Refresher as were done in the 2004 collection from the main sample.

Ryff provided response rates for the Core baseline sample and for two subsequent follow-ups, arrayed by phone interviews, questionnaires, and the cognitive project (Table 2-1). The numbers in bold at the second follow-up highlight gains in participation due to a re-fielding effort that resulted in completion of 193 questionnaires and 263 Brief Tests of Adult Cognition by Telephone (BTACTs). Ryff said she believes the incentives were important in achieving the outcomes. They included an upfront unconditional incentive of $10 plus $75 for completion of the self-administered questionnaire, and $10 up front plus $50 for completion of the BTACT.

As can be seen in the third section of Table 2-1, the response rates for the Refresher sample, recruited in 2012, were lower than the baseline of the Core sample, consistent with declining participation rates observed in

TABLE 2-1 MIDUS Response Rates

	Baseline	1st Follow-up	2nd Follow-up
Core (National)			
Phone interview	70%	75%	75%
Self-Administered Questionnaire (SAQ)	89%	81%	83(89)%**
Cognitive	NA	85%	82(90)%**
Core (Milwaukee)			
Personal interview	71%	78%	
SAQ	70%	84%	
Cognitive	52%	85%	
Refresher (National)			
Phone interview	59%		
SAQ	74%		
Cognitive	71%		
Refresher (Milwaukee)			
Personal interview	48%		
SAQ	58%		
Cognitive	42%		

NOTE: Longitudinal response rates adjusted for mortality.
** Response rates in parentheses adjusted for Refielding Effort.
SOURCE: Adapted from Carol Ryff workshop presentation, September 27, 2021.

other national surveys. MIDUS documentation shows, however, that the Refresher sample aligns well with the 2012 Current Population Survey (CPS), except for being somewhat more educated. The second and fourth sections of the table show the response rates for MIDUS recruitment of an oversample of 1,200 African Americans from Milwaukee, Wisconsin, half of whom were recruited at the second wave of the Core sample and the other half as part of the Refresher recruitment. Examples of scientific findings on racial differences in objectively measured sleep and their links to neighborhood disadvantage and cardiometabolic health were noted.

Ryff next described the Retention-Early Warning (REW) project, which was initiated to bring back participants who had dropped out of the study, given what is known from MIDUS (Radler and Ryff, 2010) and other national studies about selective attrition. The goals were to improve representativeness of the sample and also allow investigation of targeted scientific questions. She reported that 651 attritors were brought back into the study using high incentives and state-of-the-art methods from the University of Wisconsin Survey Center, with initial findings summarized in Song et al. (2021).

Concerns about respondent burden arise in MIDUS, Ryff said, because participants are asked for multiple things beyond the survey. For example, the biomarker project includes a 2-day clinic visit plus travel. Nonetheless, she emphasized high retention in the third wave from among those who had participated in multiple projects. Specifically and beyond their survey participation, 75 percent of those who previously participated in the cognitive project returned, 85 percent of those from the daily project returned, and over 90 percent returned of those who participated in the biomarker and neuroscience projects.

For the biomarker study, Ryff described efforts to overcome barriers to participation, such as providing flexible scheduling, cultivating trust by addressing participant concerns, covering all travel plus companion travel if needed, and covering other expenses such as childcare, pet care, and farm help. They also provide an incentive of $200 at the end of the visit.

MIDUS uses newsletters, which include relevant health information, sent to participant's homes as a primary way of giving back to them. Ryff shared an example of a recent Purpose in Life newsletter, which explains what purpose in life is, and shows how it matters for promoting longevity and reducing risk of various disease outcomes. Participants in the biomarker project have reported that they are participating in MIDUS because they are interested in the research, they want to contribute to science, and they appreciate the money and health information received.

MIDUS has separate informed consents for each project, some of which have multiple consents within them, the text of which is largely determined by the Institutional Review Boards (IRBs). The IRBs dictate the language to use, much of which is about protecting the institution against legal liability.

She commented that "informed consent" is a strange phrase, given that these documents often confuse more than they inform, as illustrated by the nine-page consent form for the biomarker project. For example, the required text states: "There is no direct benefit to participating," despite the fact that participants are provided multiple types of health information. There is also text saying participants might lose their health insurance or their job if certain results get into their health record, and that if they are physically injured as a result of participating, they will receive care, but will have to pay for it.

Ryff recapped her key points on how MIDUS has achieved enhanced participation and retention by using targeted incentives within all projects, cultivating rapport through newsletters, using personal interviews in Milwaukee and the REW project, and carefully pacing requests from project to project. She concluded by noting that MIDUS data are extensively used by the scientific community from which over 1,500 publications have been generated by over 24,000 unique users. The MIDUS website provides findings across 34 different topical areas with links to PDFs of the publications.[2]

National Social Life, Health, and Aging Project (NSHAP)

Linda Waite, the George Herbert Mead Distinguished Service Professor of Sociology at the University of Chicago and senior fellow at NORC at the University of Chicago, is principal investigator of NSHAP.[3] NSHAP is a longitudinal, population-based study of health, and especially social factors and social life. The study was designed to understand the links between different components of health and well-being among older community-dwelling Americans. She noted that for the first three rounds of NSHAP, all data collection was done in person.

Waite said that Round 1 of NSHAP was fielded in 2005–2006 and recruited 3,005 completed interviews with a response rate of 75.5 percent. Round 2 in 2010–2011 attempted re-interviews with everyone from Round 1 and added spouses and cohabiting partners. The conditional response rate of the original participants was almost 90 percent, and they were also able to interview 26 percent of Round 1 nonrespondents. Round 3 took place in 2015–2016, and in addition to seeking to re-interview everyone who had been interviewed previously, they recruited a younger cohort, aged 50 to 67 years, so that the full sample had a total age range from 50 to 95 years. She noted that the conditional response rate for those who have been interviewed before was over 90 percent, and the response rate for the new cohort was 76 percent.

---

[2] See http://www.midus.wisc.edu/index.php.
[3] For more information, see https://www.norc.org/Research/Projects/Pages/national-social-life-health-and-aging-project.aspx.

Waite described the strategies to gain in-person cooperation. NSHAP provided interviewers with a leaflet and a loose-leaf binder, which included newspaper articles, examples of scientific publications, and endorsements by local government, so that the interviewers could tailor to the concerns of each respondent. All Round 1 through Round 3 interviews were done in person, and respondents were given a $100 incentive. Toward the end of the field period, NSHAP increased the incentives to obtain interviews from respondents who had already been asked several times. If a respondent's spouse had already been interviewed, both were given the higher incentive. They also sent tailored refusal letters, often by FedEx toward the end of the field period, which seemed to increase response.

Round 4, which Waite said is in the field now, has absorbed a tremendous amount of research and scientific effort over the last 3 or 4 years, and is different of necessity. Rounds 1 through 3 were all in person, and consisted of a 2-hour interview that included collection of biomeasures: blood pressure, saliva, sensory function, and physical function. That was a big challenge to conduct. The move to remote data collection (internet, telephone, and mail) is expected to be less expensive, but that is to be determined. Waite noted that remote data collection may be more appropriate for some respondents who prefer it, and it has allowed NORC to develop the tools to consider a hybrid, remote, and in-person approach now and in the future. Work on the remote protocol began prior to the COVID-19 pandemic, which meant that many of the materials were already developed and pretested, and the remote protocol has allowed them to collect data during the pandemic.

Waite described the strategy to categorize participants by their likelihood of participating remotely. The most cooperative respondents, who completed all previous rounds quickly and did not need an increased incentive, are assigned to remote data collection. The second group, which was assigned to be interviewed in person, are those whom the investigators saw as needing more handholding and being more reluctant: They may have participated in only one previous round, needed a higher incentive, or were nonrespondents in the recruitment phase for the second, younger cohort. Approximately 2,500 respondents are initially assigned to remote data collection and 2,700 respondents are assigned to be interviewed in person.

For those participants assigned to a remote mode of data collection, Waite said that they will use mail push to web, in which a request is mailed to respondents with a link to a questionnaire on the internet. Those who complete the web-based questionnaire are asked for permission to mail them a "BioBox," which is the remote biomeasure data collection, followed by a supplementary self-completion questionnaire, which is also the leave-behind questionnaire for the in-person mode. (See Chapter 4 for more information on the BioBox.)

Waite said that respondents who like the web complete the survey very quickly, so NHSAP has had tremendous success during COVID-19. If respondents do not complete the web-based questionnaire, NORC attempts to reach them via phone. If staff are able to complete the interview on the phone, then respondents are asked for consent to send the BioBox and the leave-behind questionnaire. Some people preferred a paper-and-pencil questionnaire, which they were sent in the mail. All participants interviewed in person have the biomeasures taken in person as well, and they also receive the leave-behind questionnaire.

Finally, Waite described the COVID-19 substudy, which was carried out from October 2020 to January 2021 and was funded by NIA. It was NSHAP's first attempt at remote data collection and included no biomeasures. For this study, NORC contacted all NSHAP respondents for whom they had any kind of contact information. They first asked participants to complete a survey on the internet. If they did not respond, then they were sent a paper-and-pencil questionnaire to complete and return. The final attempted contact for nonrespondents was via phone. Complete questionnaire data were obtained from approximately 2,700 respondents, which was a response rate of 58 percent.

Waite briefly described the results of a logistic regression used to examine the characteristics of nonrespondents. They found that some demographic characteristics and physical health predicted response to the survey. This information will be used in Round 4 by selecting for in-person data collection more often for respondents who are younger, not married, and in poorer health. NSHAP investigators will also consider other ways to mitigate nonresponse for men, minorities, and those with less education.

National Longitudinal Study of Adolescent to Adult Health (Add Health)

Robert Hummer, the Howard W. Odum Distinguished Professor of Sociology and Fellow of the Carolina Population Center at the University of North Carolina at Chapel Hill, is the director and principal investigator of the National Longitudinal Study of Adolescent to Adult Health (Add Health).[4] Add Health is a nationally representative study of people who were in grades 7 through 12 in the mid-1990s, and the original 20,745 individual adolescents in Wave 1 were drawn from a random sample of 80 paired (high school and feeder school) schools throughout the United States. The first four waves of Add Health, which unfolded as the adolescents went through the transition to adulthood and were young adults in 2008, were all in-person data collection efforts, and the response rates can be seen in Table 2-2.

---

[4]For more information, see https://addhealth.cpc.unc.edu/.

TABLE 2-2 Add Health Longitudinal Design

	In-School Administration	Survey Administration		Biomarker Data Collection	
Wave I 1994–1995	Students N = 90,118	School Admin N = 144	Adolescents in Grades 7–12 N = 20,745 (RR = 79.0%)	Parent N = 17,670	
Wave II 1996		School Admin N = 144	Adolescents in Grades 8–12 N = 14,738 (RR = 88.6%)		
Wave III 2001–2002		Partners N = 1,507	Transition to Adulthood Aged 18–26 N = 15,197 (RR = 77.4%)	Saliva and Urine N = 14,012	
Wave IV 2008			Young Adults Aged 24–32 N = 15,701 (RR = 80.3%)	Blood Spots N = 14,687	IIV Study N ~ 100
Wave V 2016–2018		Sexual Orientation, Gender Identity, and Health N = 2,665	Adults Aged 33–43 N = 12,300 (RR = 72.0%)	Parent N = 3,000 Venous Blood N ~ 5,381	IIV Study N ~ 100
Wave VI 2022–2024			Early Midlife Adults Aged 40–50 Goal N = 13,194 (Goal RR = 73.0%)	Venous Blood Goal N = 7,500	IIV Study N ~ 100

SOURCES: Adapted from Robert Hummer workshop presentation, September 27, 2021.

Hummer focused his presentation on the lessons learned from the transition to a predominantly web-based survey due to high costs of in-person surveying and a lower funding level for Wave V. He described how the sample of roughly 20,000 was split into three subsamples to spread data collection costs over 3 years. In Year 2, they further divided the sample into web-based and a traditional in-person interview of roughly 1,100 respondents, which was done to replicate earlier waves of Add Health as an in-person interview and to estimate mode effects. In addition, they shifted from in-person to a mixed-mode interview, which was mostly web based with a little bit of mail collection. They also sampled web and mail nonrespondents in person and interviewed them in their home on a project laptop. The questionnaire length was reduced from 90 to 50 minutes from earlier waves of Add Health because of the new web-based survey design. At the end of the survey interview, respondents were asked to consent to the home health exam. If they consented, then biological data were collected in a separate home health exam by a subcontractor.

Hummer described the results from the Wave V data collection. From the overall sample, they obtained 12,300 respondents for an effective response rate of 72 percent, which was somewhat lower than earlier waves of Add Health, which ranged from 77 to 90 percent. For the web-based samples, they successfully interviewed 52 percent, which increased to 72 percent with extensive nonresponse follow-up (see Table 2-3). Approximately 8,400 survey respondents consented to do the home health exam, which is about a 68 percent consent rate. Importantly, about 90 percent of respondents surveyed in person consented to a home health exam, whereas

TABLE 2-3 Add Health Wave 5 Response and Consent Rates

Overall sample size of 12,300 (effective response rate of 72%)	
Samples 1, 2A, 3 (n = 11,198)	
Web/Mail response rate:	52.0%
Nonresponse follow-up response rate:	41.3%
Combined response rate:	71.8%
Sample 2B (n = 1,102)	
In-person response rate:	72.2%
Consented 8,379 (of 12,300) survey respondents for home health exam (68%)	
Consent rate ~90% among in-person survey respondents	
Consent rate ~60% among web/mail-based respondents	
Conducted 5,381 exams (of 8,379 consented)… (64%)	

SOURCE: Adapted from Robert Hummer workshop presentation, September 27, 2021.

only 60 percent who took the survey largely via web consented to the exam. However, they were only able to conduct about 5,400 home health exams, due to scheduling difficulties and no-shows. More detailed information on the Wave V methods can be found in Biemer et al. (forthcoming) and Harris et al. (2019).

Hummer summarized the 12 lessons learned from Wave V about the survey methods:

1. A 50-to-60-minute web survey is feasible. They tested breaking it up into 25-minute segments but found that allowing people to rest or finish another day was not necessary; respondents wanted to complete it all at once.
2. The mail option was costly and yielded poorer data than the web.
3. Having an email address was a key factor for both web and in-person response.
4. Constant reminders were important. They left the web-based survey open for a year or even longer and mailed out postcards, letters, and, toward the end, FedEx mailers.
5. The in-person response rate of about 72 percent continues to be higher than the web, which was about 52 percent. Responses via the web were much cheaper: about one-tenth the cost of an in-person survey.
6. Any national news about data breaches or confidentiality hurts survey response.
7. The nonresponse follow-up was very important in achieving a more representative sample. They subsampled nonrespondents and devoted considerable resources to the nonresponse follow-up operations.
8. Higher incentives matter, but it was not a complete solution.
9. Parents were not helpful in finding their children in Add Health; they were more likely to protect the confidentiality of their children than to provide their address.
10. Many respondents reported high regard for participation in Add Health, and they said they want to contribute to science and see it as a very important research effort.
11. There were some mode effects in switching from in-person to web survey.
12. The rate of in-person respondents' consent for the home exam was much higher than that of web or mail-based respondents, which is one of the downsides of moving to a web-based survey.

Hummer described plans for Wave VI, which is now in development with fieldwork anticipated to begin in May 2022. They are planning to go back to the entire sample, administering a web-based survey to approximately three-fourths of the sample, and an in-person survey to the remaining quarter. Special measures on sensory, physical, and cognitive functioning will be collected for the in-person sample. Each of the two samples will be nationally representative and, importantly for the web-based survey sample, an in-person nonresponse follow-up will go after critically needed nonrespondents.

Hummer noted the ambitious response rate goals for Wave VI: they are projecting a 67 percent raw response rate, a conditional consent rate for exams of 74 percent, and a conditional rate of 77 percent for completing the exams from those who consented. He pointed out many lessons were learned from Wave V regarding how to do a web survey, how to transition from an in-person to a web survey, and so forth. They plan to conduct more intensive panel maintenance with newsletters and tracing activities in order to continue to update addresses and send notifications to sample members. They also have shorter periodicity between Waves V and VI, compared to Waves IV and V, which was a period of 8 to 9 years when they did not conduct interviews. Larger survey incentives in Wave VI compared with Wave V are offered, as well as a larger and high-density targeted nonresponse follow-up for nonrespondents to selectively go after the types of people less likely to respond to a web-based survey. Finally, a larger in-person subsample with oversamples of racial and ethnic minorities will be conducted to obtain data on sensory, physical, and cognitive functioning.

The consent processes for the survey consist of a description written at a very low reading level, Hummer explained. They assess the respondent's capacity to provide informed consent with a brief series of questions, and then they collect an electronic signature. They plan to collect additional consents for the home exam and the potential for future linkages to Medicare/Medicaid data and educational data through the last four digits of a respondent's Social Security Number. Planning is under way to increase the incentive for the home exam and to ask respondents both at the beginning and at the end of the survey if they will consent to the home exam, not just at the end.

The Health and Retirement Study (HRS)

David Weir, research professor in the Survey Research Center at the Institute for Social Research at the University of Michigan, is the director of the Health and Retirement Study (HRS).[5] Weir started by showing the growth in publications that use the HRS to underscore that the reason to care about response and consent is the science that can be created from the

---

[5]For more information, see https://hrsonline.isr.umich.edu/.

data collected. Figure 2-1 shows the response rate to the HRS interviews, which have been administered every other year beginning in 1992. The 15th wave was completed in 2020. Starting in 2014, response rates greatly declined. However, Weir stated, responses rates alone do not show what is happening. He illustrated this in Figure 2-2, with a series of effort-yield curves that have an index for the number of attempts along the horizontal axis, with response rates on the vertical axis. These curves show that the same number of contact attempts results in lower and lower response rates from 2006 on, and that it takes more and more total attempts to reach the same response rate as the last wave; moreover, starting in 2014 the final response rates were slightly lower than the previous wave despite increasing total attempts. Weir also noted that in 2018 and 2020, budget cuts forced limits on the effort. They stopped at a fewer number of attempts than in previous waves and had a noticeably lower response rate. In 2020, the pandemic required converting in-person interviews to phone, but they were able to make more telephone calls and increase the number of attempts about as far as they did in 2016. Weir noted that if the number of attempts had not increased since 2006, the response rate in 2020 would have been about 12 points lower than it was.

Weir provided an overview of what they have learned about nonresponse bias and selection effects. The decline in participation has been

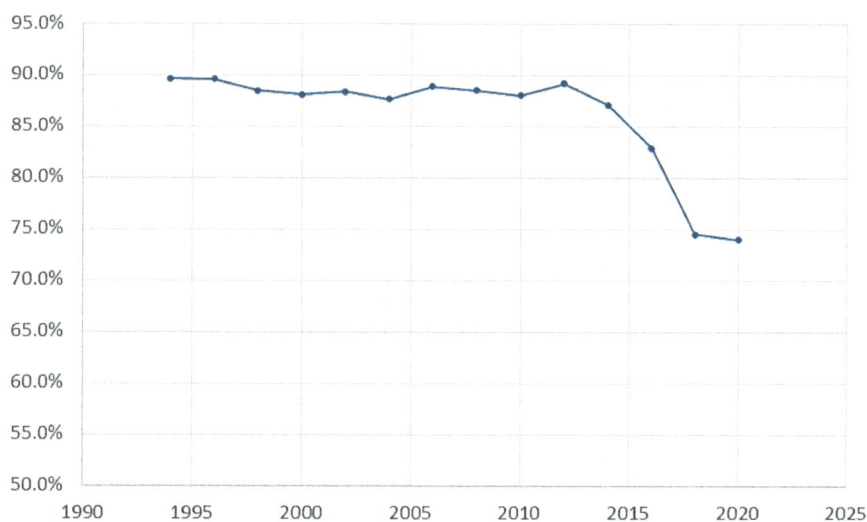

FIGURE 2-1 Core interview response rates for the Health and Retirement Study, 1994–2020.
SOURCE: David Weir workshop presentation, September 27, 2021.

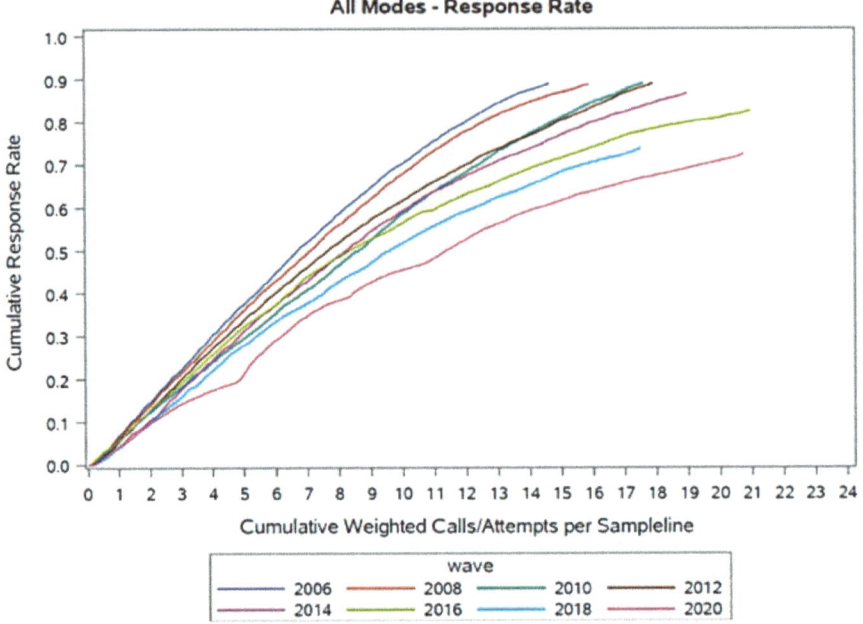

FIGURE 2-2 Cumulative responses by wave and effort (cumulative number of call attempts).
SOURCE: David Weir workshop presentation, September 27, 2021.

more prevalent in the White sample than in the minority sample. Blacks have higher response rates than Whites, and Hispanics have about the same response rates as Whites. They have also seen a trend toward lower response rates among less-educated participants, which has grown in the most recent waves. Incentive payments to respondents have increased over time. The payments are a little higher for the in-person than for the telephone interviews, which are $80 for the core interview and another $20 for the in-person interview that also has a leave-behind questionnaire.

Weir described analyses comparing interviewers and the number of attempts it took to get an interview in 2006 and 2018. Interviewers today are more representative of the whole population, and there is more variance in performance across interviewers. However, he reiterated, the main finding is that the whole distribution has shifted toward requiring many more attempts per interview for nearly all interviewers such that even the best interviewers of today do not do as well as the worst interviewers of 15 years ago. He also noted that the length of interviews rose steadily from 2000 to 2012, and in 2014 they made a conscious effort to reduce length.

It increased some in 2016, but has been flat since then. They have also asked respondents to complete mail surveys, and these surveys have shown a similar pattern of decline in response over time.

Weir turned to consent rates for biological samples. Saliva samples are collected for the purpose of getting DNA, and consent rates have been quite stable between 80 and 85 percent. Respondents are asked for consent as part of the in-person interview, and the sample is collected right after they sign the consent. If a participant does not consent, the interviewers ask again in a subsequent wave, and an additional 5 percent does consent. The second request is also helpful in bringing consent rates for Blacks to be more similar to rates for Whites and Hispanics.

Dried blood spots are collected as part of that same in-person interview, Weir continued, and more recently they have been doing whole blood collection. They have seen lower consent rates among Blacks to provide blood samples than Whites or Hispanics. The blood draws are done by a separate contractor, which means that people can refuse to consent at the time of the interview, and they can also refuse when the contractor comes to take their blood, so the overall rate for blood collections is about two-thirds of the sample.

Weir also described how respondents' consent is sought to link to Medicare records, and those who decline are asked again in subsequent waves. Linkage consent rates have been declining but multiple requests help considerably in raising rates. Blacks are slightly less likely to agree to linking their data to Medicare records, and there is a tendency for the most educated to consent at slightly higher rates.

Weir concluded by noting that they have conducted in-home cognitive assessments to identify dementia, which is a high-priority issue for NIA. An initial expensive in-home assessment took place about 20 years ago and obtained about a 56 percent response rate. Development of a Harmonized Cognitive Assessment Protocol has since proved to be much less expensive and much less burdensome for respondents, and they obtained a 79 percent response rate in 2016.

Discussion

Vetta Thompson began the discussion by asking about the adequacy of funding for continuing to improve or even maintain response rates. Weir pointed out two paths. As part of the puzzle, the first, using the web for data collection, offers low-cost ways of gathering information, but has lower participation. Adjustment can be made to keep web collection representative, so it is a potential path. The other path, he said, is very intensive in-person contact to try to boost participation and response, which is a much more expensive undertaking and may not be feasible with large sample studies.

Thompson next asked the presenters' views on the most effective way to keep the representativeness of the sample and attend to the needs of the science. Hummer replied that for Add Health, moving to the large web-based survey has been very helpful both because it costs so much less than traditional in-person interviews and it provides a way to get information from the most cooperative respondents. Then they spend more of their resources trying to fill in their sample with those most needed to maintain representativeness. That was Add Health's strategy for Wave V and is planned for Wave VI. He noted, however, that they have not solved the issue of lower consent for home exams via web than in-person interviews.

IDENTIFYING AND REDUCING SELECTION BIAS

Measuring and Reducing Nonresponse and Linkage Nonconsent Bias

Joe Sakshaug, distinguished researcher at the German Institute for Employment Research, professor of statistics at the Ludwig Maximilian University of Munich, and honorary professor in the School of Social Sciences at the University of Mannheim, began his presentation noting that it is important to look at the conceptual pathway to selection. The typical start is with a gross sample drawn from a frame or administrative database. Some sample members are respondents and some are nonrespondents, which constitutes the first stage of selection. Usually only a subset of respondents give their consent for data linkage or biomarkers. Even among those who consent to the linkage or biomarkers, only a smaller subset can be linked or, as Weir also mentioned, only a subset of those who consent actually have their blood drawn. So, he noted, at least two, maybe more, levels of selection must be considered when identifying and analyzing selection bias. He extended this consideration to the panel framework where a panel survey may be collecting data over multiple time points. He said that nonresponse can occur at each wave of data collection: some sample members may participate in one or two waves and then drop out, so the cumulative nonresponse tends to increase over time.

Sakshaug noted that to identify and correct for both consent and response biases, it is useful to have auxiliary data available, such as administrative data, frame data, paradata, or commercial data. In the longitudinal case, previous wave survey data can be potentially useful for identifying and correcting for nonresponse bias. In the case of linkage nonconsent, he commented, it is useful to have any of the above auxiliary data sources, as well as current wave survey data.

Sakshaug described studies where he looked at the magnitude of nonresponse bias and linkage nonconsent bias. In the first study (Sakshaug and Kreuter, 2012), he and his colleague examined linkage nonconsent bias, nonresponse bias, and measurement bias in a mixed-mode survey of welfare benefit recipients in Germany by using administrative records. Because they did not need linkage consent in order to link the administrative records, they could ask for consent and then use the administrative data to assess differences between consenters and nonconsenters. The consent rate was about 78 percent (Table 2-4), and nonconsent bias was the lesser of the problems when compared to other traditional sources of survey error, like nonresponse bias and measurement bias. They discovered some significant nonconsent biases for age and for foreign citizenship, but these were quite small relative to measurement bias and nonresponse bias. Measurement bias tended to be the largest source of error compared to nonresponse and nonconsent, and slightly more variables showed nonresponse biases compared to nonconsent biases.

In the second study (Sakshaug and Huber, 2016), he and his colleague examined nonconsent bias and panel nonresponse bias in a longitudinal study of employees in Germany. Looking at the average bias across several characteristics taken from administrative records, they found that panel nonresponse bias tends to be the more dominant source of bias. The average relative nonconsent bias was quite low, which was not surprising since the consent rate in this study was around 90 percent. Nonconsent dropped slightly over time because the respondents who did not consent in the previous wave were asked again and some of them consented in the following waves.

Sakshaug highlighted several research studies on adjusting for panel nonresponse bias. The first study (Silverwood et al., 2020) used previous wave survey data to adjust for panel nonresponse. The authors applied a data-driven multiple imputation approach for nonresponse bias adjustment in the Next Steps Cohort Study, using the previous seven waves of data.

TABLE 2-4 CATI/CAPI Cross-Sectional Survey of Welfare Benefit Recipients in Germany (administrative records available for drawn sample)

Characteristics	Nonresponse Bias	Nonconsent Bias	Measurement Bias
Age (years)	0.1	−0.3*	−0.0
Foreign (%)	−5.6*	−0.9*	−2.5*
Unemployment benefit (%)	3.2*	−0.3	−7.5*
Disability (%)	0.4	0.0	6.1*
Employment status (%)	1.0	0.3	−1.0
Monthly income (EUR)	−71.4*	1.7	402.4*

NOTE: * $p<0.05$.
SOURCE: Adapted from Joe Sakshaug workshop presentation, September 27, 2021, from Sakshaug and Kreuter (2012).

They drew upon over 850 eligible predictor variables from earlier waves and imputed nonresponse in the previous seven waves of data collection, applied a variable selection method to identify significant predictors of the Wave 8 nonresponse, and then used these retained predictors to multiply impute the Wave 8 outcomes. Table 2-5 shows results before and after the multiple imputation (MI). The far-right columns show nonresponse bias in these selected characteristics, but after applying the multiple imputation approach, the authors did see some bias reduction in these variables.

Sakshaug next described how to use administrative data in a piggyback longitudinal study to adjust for nonresponse bias. Piggyback longitudinal surveys recruit their participants from a separate, independent cross-sectional survey. Examples include the Medical Expenditure Panel Survey (MEPS) Household Component, which draws its sample from the U.S. National Health Interview Survey. According to Sakshaug, many cross-sectional surveys used in piggyback longitudinal studies perform administrative record linkages, provided that the respondent gives consent to those linkages. He wanted to explore whether it is possible to use these existing linkages from cross-sectional surveys to measure and adjust for nonresponse bias in these piggyback longitudinal surveys. He noted challenges to this approach because not all cross-sectional respondents are willing to participate in the follow-up survey, and not all of them consent to linkage, so further adjustments for these different sources of selection must be made.

Sakshaug briefly referred to a study (Büttner et al., 2021) that has found several administrative variables that were significant predictors of participation in each of the waves of the longitudinal survey. Current and

TABLE 2-5 Adjusting for Panel Nonresponse Bias Using Previous Wave(s) Survey Data

Characteristics	Wave 1 Rs	Wave 8 Rs		NR Bias	
		Complete case analysis	MI approach	Before MI	After MI
Male (%)	51.5	45.0	46.6	−6.5	−4.9
Non-White British (%)	14.1	12.8	14.3	−1.3	0.2
Single parent household (%)	23.5	19.5	23.3	4.0	−0.2
Ever suspended (%)	11.1	7.3	10.5	−3.85	−0.6
Attend university (%)	36.9*	44.5	38.2	7.6	1.3
Income (GBP)	33,022	34,756	32,673	1734	−349

NOTE: *External benchmark (estimated).
SOURCE: Adapted from Joe Sakshaug workshop presentation, September 27, 2021, from Silverwood et al. (2020).

between-wave information was associated with attrition, and incorporating these linked-administrative data in the weighting adjustment reduced nonresponse bias for some variables.

Sakshaug concluded by discussing survey design strategies for reducing nonconsent bias. He described studies that have experimented with the placement of the linkage consent question and noted that most of these studies find that asking for linkage consent at the beginning or at least in the middle of the survey has a higher consent rate than asking at the end. Linkage consent biases exist, he said, but are small relative to nonresponse biases, and using rich survey and linked-administrative data are useful for measuring and adjusting for nonresponse bias. He reiterated that linkage consent rates can be improved by asking for consent at the beginning of the questionnaire, as opposed to the end.

Identifying and Mitigating Nonresponse in a Longitudinal Survey of the Medicare Population

Debra Reed-Gillette is director of the Survey Management and Analytics Group (SMAG) within the Office of Enterprise Data and Analytics (OEDA) of the Centers for Medicare & Medicaid Services (CMS), and she is the director of the current Medicare Current Beneficiary Survey (MCBS). Reed-Gillette began by providing background on the MCBS and the strategies used since 2015 to mitigate nonresponse and to ensure the sample is representative of the Medicare population.

MCBS is a continuous, in-person longitudinal survey representing Medicare beneficiaries aged 65 and over and beneficiaries who are under age 65 who are eligible for Medicare due to disabling conditions, Reed-Gillette explained. The MCBS is used in administering the Medicare program, monitoring and evaluating beneficiary health status, and understanding how the health care policies affect the beneficiaries. The survey has been conducted since 1991, and each survey is interviewed up to three times per calendar year for four consecutive years in a rotating panel design to form a continuous profile of their health care experiences. One panel is retired during each winter round and a new panel is selected to replace those who have retired each fall round.

According to Reed-Gillette, an important feature of the MCBS is its ability to link self-reported data with administrative claims and enrollment data that are available with the Medicare program, which permits an examination of both the health care characteristics of beneficiaries and health care cost and utilization. The MCBS also includes facility-residing beneficiaries, and beneficiaries are followed who go into and out of long-term care facilities and skilled nursing facilities to maintain a comprehensive profile of their health care utilization expenditures and their changes and transitions through the health care system. Finally, the MCBS includes an oversample of beneficiaries who are Hispanic, who have disabling conditions, who are age 64 and under, and who are age 85 and over to have sufficient sample sizes for analyses of those groups. The sample is selected to be representative of all Medicare enrollees, including enrollees during the current benefit year, and consists of 16,000 respondents annually.

Because they have administrative data on Medicare enrollment, Reed-Gillette said that the demographics of the Medicare population can be compared to the survey respondents. Differential nonresponse can impede observation of change over time in subgroups, degrade the representativeness of the sample, and have a lasting impact across the study for longitudinal analyses, she reported. Several techniques have been used during fielding of the survey to help identify and mitigate this differential nonresponse. They also have conducted a nonresponse bias analysis every 3 years to identify any additional impacts and to determine potential mitigation strategies.

For the most recent round, Reed-Gillette said, the overall response rate was 80.5 percent; the incoming 2020 panel sample had a response rate of 75.3 percent, and the continuing panel had a response rate of 85.1 percent. Once respondents are in the survey for at least two rounds, they almost always continue for all 4 years.

Reed-Gillette described how they are using R-indicators to look at representativeness of respondents, in addition to response rates, to examine the variability of subgroup response rates during data collection. The R-indicators are computed from response propensities modeled using variables on the sample frame, including race, sex, age, ethnicity, stratum, and region of the country. They examine the variability and the changes in these propensities over the rounds of data collection. They also look at weekly response rates as well as R-indicator reports and provide this information to field managers, so that interviewer case priorities can be adjusted if needed during fielding to target respondent groups in need of increased responses and participation. In her presentation slides, Reed-Gillette provided examples of the dashboards shared with field interviewers that highlight the characteristics of respondents that require more targeted interviewing efforts.

Reed-Gillette also pointed to improvements in locating strategies to reduce nonresponse by using administrative and commercial data sources, which may be more up-to-date than the addresses from enrollment information. Administrative data from assessments that are required from Medicare and Medicaid certified facilities can help locate individuals who have been in facilities by using those administrative assessment records.

Contacting strategies are also improving, Reed-Gillette said. The language of the advance letter sent to beneficiaries has been revised to directly and clearly ask the beneficiary to participate in the survey. The signatory of the letter has been changed to the survey director, rather than the CMS privacy officer, which improved respondents' understanding of who was asking them to participate. The logos on the letterhead and envelopes were reviewed to make sure the letter looks legitimate, which has helped reduce nonresponse. Reed-Gillette also described coordination with Social Security and within the Medicare program itself to ensure that the MCBS is legitimate in the eyes of respondents. They have provided information on the survey to the 1-800 Medicare hotline, because many respondents will call to determine whether or not the advance letter is indeed legitimate or a scam. They have also provided information to Social Security Offices because beneficiaries may contact them about the legitimacy of the survey.

In conclusion, Reed-Gillette described a new study in the field examining beneficiary response to various types of reminder letters. They are comparing having no reminder with a FedEx reminder, a regular mail letter, or a postcard. The early information is showing that the FedEx reminder is most effective with increased call volume to the respondent 1-800 number and hits on a responsive website shortly after receipt of the FedEx package. Completion rate for the FedEx reminder has been almost 10 percentage points higher than through other contact attempts. Another study will look at the types of materials sent to beneficiaries because they have found that glossy materials are considered to be less official and appear more like marketing. They plan to compare a one-page set of frequently asked questions about the survey to a shiny, glossy brochure. Reed-Gillette provided a link to the MCBS website for more information about the survey.[6]

Informing Follow-up Strategies to Reduce Nonresponse Bias

Andy Peytchev is a senior survey methodologist and fellow at RTI. He began by discussing the similarities between longitudinal surveys and cross-sectional surveys. Most of the nonresponse occurs in the first wave of data collection, he commented, and that is the similarity with any survey. In terms of representativeness, the first wave of data collection in a longitudinal design probably has the greatest potential for nonresponse bias because of the amount of nonresponse. Peytchev explained the bias in an estimate of a mean is the difference between a respondent and a nonrespondent mean multiplied by the nonresponse rate. Therefore, he pointed out, when the nonresponse rate is large, even relatively small differences between respondents and nonrespondents could lead to biases of substantive importance. Another similarity between cross-sectional surveys and the first wave in longitudinal surveys is that there is typically not much information

---

[6] For more information, see www.cms.gov/mcbs.

available for nonrespondents. He noted that there has been a lot of research on cross-sectional surveys that is relevant to longitudinal surveys for the first wave of data collection.

In terms of dissimilarities, which was the focus of the rest of his presentation, Peytchev noted that longitudinal surveys have a wealth of substantive information collected in the early waves of data collection, and those variables are often related to measurements in subsequent waves. Therefore, the researcher could use the information collected in the first wave to measure bias after that first wave of data collection, inform data collection efforts after the first wave, and inform the nonresponse adjustments. Peytchev clarified that the measurement of bias after the initial wave assumes that the variables are stable over time, but this is not the bias researchers are interested in because the longitudinal design is usually used to measure change over time. Thus, the researcher will not have information on the estimates of change from the survey. He noted that there is more potential for using information, such as paradata and substantive data from prior waves to inform and tailor the data collection, for example by building models to identify which respondents would contribute to greater bias if they do not respond to the next wave. Finally, he noted that there is a wider array of variables that could be used for nonresponse adjustments.

Peytchev described two case studies to illustrate how longitudinal studies benefit from using the initial data collected to inform later data collections to reduce the risk of nonresponse bias. The first case study was a field test for the Baccalaureate and Beyond Longitudinal Study (B&B), which is a piggyback survey because it consists of a sample of respondents to the National Postsecondary Student Aid Study (NPSAS). NPSAS is like Wave 1 of a longitudinal study and B&B is the follow-up study that is done afterwards as a longitudinal study, Peytchev commented. The field test used three protocols (Table 2-6). All the protocols began with web data collection. The default protocol included CATI interviewing that started several weeks into data collection, offered an abbreviated interview to convert nonrespondents, and provided a $30 incentive for completion. The relaxed protocol simply offered a $20 incentive for web completion; there was no telephone interviewing or offer of an abbreviated interview. The aggressive protocol initiated CATI interviewing much earlier (week 2), included a $10 prepaid incentive and an additional $20 for completion, and offered an abbreviated interview earlier as well (week 4).

Respondents were assigned to the different protocols based on paradata from the prior data collection, NPSAS. The first group are the early respondents in NPSAS, the second group are late respondents to NPSAS, and Groups 3 and 4 are the nonrespondents to NPSAS, who were randomly split into two groups with half receiving the default protocol and half the aggressive protocol.

TABLE 2-6 Treatments Used in 2016/2017 Baccalaureate and Beyond Longitudinal Study (B&B) Field Test

Phase	Relaxed	Default	Aggressive
Early Completion			Prepaid incentive CATI interviewing (week 2)
Production	No CATI contact	CATI interviewing (week 5)	Offer abbreviated interview (week 4)
Nonresponse Conversion	No abbreviated interview	Offer abbreviated interview	
Incentives	$20 completion	$30 promised	$10 prepaid $20 promised

SOURCE: Adapted from Andy Peytchev workshop presentation, September 27, 2021.

Peytchev noted that the response rate for Group 1, who were the early respondents to NPSAS, was 75 percent, which was the highest response rate with the least effort (Table 2-7). Group 2, the late respondents in NPSAS, achieved a slightly lower response rate at 70 percent. Group 3, nonrespondents to NPSAS, proved to be really difficult respondents, and they had a 25 percent response rate. Group 4, also nonrespondents to NPSAS but who received a more aggressive protocol, had a substantially increased response rate compared to Group 3, with 37 percent.

Peytchev pointed out the importance of this approach in terms of bias (Table 2-7). For Groups 1 and 2, there was relatively little bias based on the available information. In contrast, Group 3 had the greatest bias, which was reduced in Group 4 using the aggressive protocol. Peytchev said it was

TABLE 2-7 Results from 2016/2017 Baccalaureate and Beyond Longitudinal Study (B&B) Field Test

Group	Response Rate	Average Absolute Relative Bias
Group 1: Early Respondents, relaxed protocol	75%	4%
Group 2: Late Respondents, default protocol	70%	5%
Group 3: Nonrespondents, default protocol	25%	18%
Group 4: Nonrespondents, aggressive protocol	37%	14%

SOURCE: Adapted from Andy Peytchev workshop presentation, September 27, 2021.

worth spending additional effort based on paradata on prior behavior to reduce overall bias.

Peytchev briefly touched on the second case study due to time constraints, but he noted that the goal was to estimate bias based on data collected from the prior wave, and use it to identify cases who not only respond at the lower rate, but also are different and underrepresented. The example he provided was a survey of renters and owners with multiple waves of data collection. Groups were defined by both response propensity and the values from prior waves. Peytchev showed that the targeted groups who were different and predicted to respond at a lower rate did have lower response rates. They were able to get those groups' participation to mimic the rest of the groups with an increased incentive, although they were not as effective in reducing nonresponse bias. Peytchev commented when change over time is correlated with nonresponse, it is about the worst situation for a longitudinal study, and that may be what is happening. He concluded by noting that increases in nonresponse requires more complex study designs, and the longitudinal studies provide more information for these designs; however, it is a new challenge to estimate change in these behaviors and desired responses to measure in subsequent waves.

Discussion

John Phillips asked the presenters about administrative data sources that are potentially relevant for U.S. longitudinal studies to reduce nonresponse bias in NIA-supported studies. He asked if the only legitimate option is something like the Social Security Numident file or whether commercial data are a good option. Reed-Gillette said her study updates data with Medicare Social Security enrollment data to have the most recent information to contact samples.

Jennifer Madans asked the presenters about the most promising areas for future research for identifying and reducing selection bias and whether research could be coordinated to build a more comprehensive knowledge base. Sakshaug posited that administrative data have a lot to offer in terms of identifying and adjusting for selection bias in panel surveys. He noted that in Germany, most administrative records are also longitudinal in nature, so that even after panel participants drop out of a study, they can be followed through the administrative records. With these data, researchers can see if panel participants who drop out go on to have very different life course patterns compared to those who stay in the surveys, which is especially relevant for measuring change. Peytchev said a lot more could be done from a responsive and adaptive survey design perspective with data in longitudinal studies. He added that administrative data could be particularly useful in weighting adjustments to improve the quality of the survey estimates themselves. Reed-Gillette said with the MCBS and the availability of the administrative data, they design the survey and the linkage with the study in mind to improve estimates of the utilization and costs of the health care services. She also said that MCBS is not allowed to use incentives, but they are interested in experimenting with them.

3

Participation

This chapter summarizes the presentations and discussion in two sessions (one on September 27, the second on September 28) that focused on survey participation. Michael Davern chaired the first session on Maximizing Respondent Retention, and Sunita Sah chaired the second session on Participant Engagement: Insights from Behavioral Science Research.

MAXIMIZING RESPONDENT RETENTION

Maximizing Response: The HILDA Survey Experience

Nicole Watson, a survey methodologist and associate professor at the Melbourne Institute within the University of Melbourne, has worked on the Household, Income and Labor Dynamics in Australia (HILDA) Survey since 2000.[1] The HILDA Survey had 7,700 responding households in Wave 1 in 2001, and added an extra 2,100 households in Wave 11 in 2011. HILDA interviews everyone in the household age 15 and older, conducting interviews with around 17,000 people each wave. For a two-adult household, the interviews take 85 minutes total. About 90 percent of interviews are done face-to-face and 10 percent are done by telephone. Interviewers also ask respondents to do a self-completion questionnaire. Fieldwork starts in July and runs until February. Incentives have changed over time, but it is currently about $45 U.S.

---

[1] For more information, see https://www.dss.gov.au/our-responsibilities/families-and-children/programmes-services/the-household-income-and-labour-dynamics-in-australia-hilda-survey.

Watson provided a figure showing re-interview rates achieved in the HILDA Survey. Figure 3-1 shows the portion of respondents in one wave re-interviewed in the next wave by 5-year age groups; deaths and people who move abroad have been removed. She noted that, similar to other panel surveys, the first few waves have higher attrition and a lower rate of re-interviews. For example, the first black line in Figure 3-1, which are 15- to 19-year-olds in Wave 1, shows that 80 percent of this group were re-interviewed in Wave 2. By Wave 5 they were re-interviewing 95 percent of the previous wave respondents within that age cohort. Among respondents in their 50s through early 70s, the re-interview rate is around 96 to 98 percent by Wave 5.

Watson described the results of research looking at hard-to-get cases. They examined whether the hard-to-get cases who are interviewed are different from the other interviewed cases; whether the cases that require a lot of effort in one survey wave require a lot of effort in all survey waves; and whether easy-to-get cases can be re-weighted to eliminate the biases that arise from not interviewing the hard-to-get cases. Hard-to-get survey respondents were found to be distinctly different from the easy-to-get cases; however, 80 to 90 percent of those hard-to-get cases are easy to get in the next wave. Watson said that they could curtail the fieldwork without noticeably affecting the population estimates if they kept the number of calls to households to 12, and the biases that were introduced by doing that could

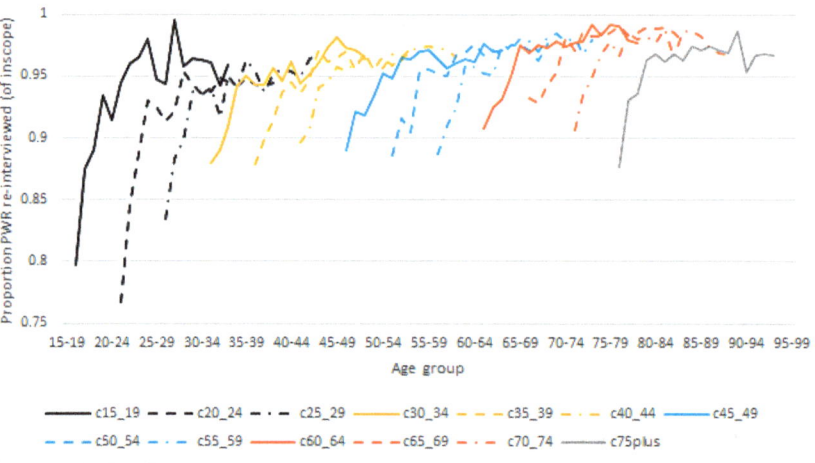

FIGURE 3-1 Proportion of previous wave respondents who were re-interviewed at each wave shown separately by age group.
SOURCES: Nicole Watson workshop presentation, September 27, 2021; data from the Household, Income and Labour Dynamics in Australia (HILDA) Survey.

be rectified through weighting. Curtailing other field activities resulted in greater cost savings. However, there were impacts on population estimates and estimates of change that were not well addressed by weighting.

Watson described another study that looked at how to re-engage previous wave nonrespondents using the HILDA Survey together with the British Household Panel Survey and the German Socioeconomic Panel. Around one-quarter of HILDA Survey nonrespondents are converted to being interviewed at each wave, she noted. The study examined different aspects of their survey fieldwork to see what encouraged people who are nonrespondents to come back and what encouraged people to continue participating from one wave to the next.

Watson highlighted the results (Table 3-1). As an example of what was learned, she pointed to the first line of the table, which shows that having the same interviewer for a person who was previously a nonrespondent has a negative effect on their likelihood of responding again but a positive effect on retaining participants from the previous wave. Watson said, therefore, they want to change the interviewer for nonrespondents but keep the same interviewer for previous respondents. The only measure that has a positive effect for both groups was to interview face-to-face rather than by phone.

Focusing on re-engaging nonrespondents, Watson noted that the longer since the last interview, the less likely these nonrespondents will return; refusals are harder to convert than other reasons for nonresponse; if the sample member changed address, that change in the household could result in a new situation that made them more amenable to being interviewed;

TABLE 3-1 Results of Different Data Collection Procedures and Events on Re-engaging Nonrespondents and Continuing Participation of Respondents

	Re-engaging nonrespondents	Continuing participation
Interviewer-respondent continuity	Negative	Positive
Change in survey mode	No effect	Negative
Face-to-face (vs phone)	Positive	Positive
Long time since last interview	Negative	n/a
Refusal (vs other reason for nonresponse)	Negative	n/a
Partial household response	No effect	Negative
Change of address	Positive	Negative
Experienced (vs new) interviewer if changed and no change of address	Positive	No effect

SOURCES: Adapted from Nicole Watson workshop presentation, September 27, 2021.

and if an interviewer has to be changed, sending an experienced interviewer convinced more nonrespondents to re-engage than sending a less experienced interviewer.

In summary, Watson said that chasing hard-to-get cases in the HILDA Survey is worthwhile, because hard-to-get is not a persistent state, people tend to fall into the hard-to-get situation temporarily, and they will become generally easy-to-get in future waves. The hard-to-get cases are distinctly different from the easy-to-get cases, and weighting does not always correct for the biases in the estimates, especially when looking at estimates of change. She noted that re-engaging nonrespondents is a different decision than continuing participation, and different factors affect re-engagement versus continued participation. She suggested considering the feasibility of changing interviewers, although it is not always possible. The next best thing, she said, would be to arm the interviewers with a toolkit that provides them with a number of fresh approaches to the household, giving them different material to present to the sample member. She also suggested trying to re-engage the sample members as soon as possible, and that when respondents move, that can be a good opportunity to re-engage.

Panel Attrition in High School and Beyond

Eric Grodsky is professor of sociology and educational policy studies at the University of Wisconsin-Madison and co-principal investigator (PI) of the High School & Beyond Midlife Follow-up Study (HS&B FU). Rachel Canas is a senior research director in the Health Sciences Department at NORC at the University of Chicago, where she currently serves as the assistant project director for HS&B FU. Grodsky began by saying an advantage that HS&B FU has for understanding selection and response in surveys of aging is that sample members were contacted a long time ago as adolescents. The adolescents were also clustered in high schools, which provides additional understanding of who does and does not continue to participate in studies as time goes by. They also have standardized assessments of academic achievement and cognitive skill in adolescence, which lets them evaluate the relationship between prior cognitive skills and attrition, a process especially relevant for studies designed to understand cognitive change, cognitive decline, onset of Alzheimer's, and Alzheimer's disease-related dementias.

Grodsky said that the target population for HS&B was students enrolled in 10th or 12th grades in the United States in the 1979–1980 school years, so they were born between 1961 and 1964. In the clustered sample design, 1,122 schools were selected for the sample and 1,105 participated (with replacement), including public schools, nonreligious private schools, and religious private schools. The schools were oversampled to make sure there were adequate numbers of Cuban-serving public and Catholic schools, other Hispanic schools, Black Catholic schools, and other non-Catholic private schools. From each school a maximum of 36 seniors and 36 sophomores were selected for the base year, and 84 percent of the sampled students are included in the data for that first year. The initial interviews were conducted in 1980.

Grodsky noted that the focus of the study is on attrition from the panel that was selected from the 1980 base year sample in 1982, and that panel included about 12,000 seniors and about 14,830 sophomores. This panel was followed up in 2014–2015 when the sample members were typically 50 to 55 years of age. They removed those who were out of sample due to mortality, illness, or institutionalization, but these sample members are carefully considered in the substantive work done on mortality as well as the nature of the surviving sample.

The attrition analyses did not distinguish among active refusals, passive refusals, and locating problems, Grodsky said. Predictors were the social background of participants, including sex, race/ethnicity, and socioeconomic status. He noted that the socioeconomic status variable was a combination of father's occupation, father's and mother's education, family income, and the presence of household items such as books. Measures of academic achievement were also used, specifically math test scores and self-reported grades in the senior year of high school. They also used the school mean math scores, centering student math scores around the school mean to distinguish between differences in attrition that could be associated with differences in the types of schools students attended and differences related to the students' own performance relative to their peers in schools.

The results of the analyses showed that women were more likely than men to respond by 6 percentage points, and relative to non-Hispanic White respondents, Black, Latinx, and respondents of other races were about 5 to 7 percentage points less likely to respond. Students who reported earning lower grades in high school were less likely to respond to the survey 35 years later, with the difference between those reporting earning A's responding 6 percentage points higher than those reporting earning B's and C's, and 16 percentage points higher than those who reported earning D's or below. Math test scores predicted participating in the survey at mid-life with each standard deviation increase in math test scores associated with about a 6 percentage point increase in the probability of response. In addition, each standard deviation increase in the school average socioeconomic status (SES) increases the probability of response by 2.8 percentage points. Within schools, there is a 1.9 percentage point bump for students for each standard deviation higher than they are relative to the school mean SES. So, he concluded, both the school mean and individual SES contribute a little bit to the probability of response in 2014–2015.

Grodsky reflected on the results and stated that these differences speak to the challenges to consider in thinking about the distribution of early life cognitive skills and noncognitive skills among people contacted later in life. He concluded by noting that in addition to the biases he described, there is also panel conditioning bias that biases the sample members who are observed over time.

Canas described how the study team took into account what they learned in previous rounds to encourage participation for a new round of data collection in 2021. They do extensive pre-field locating efforts on HS&B FU panel members because they cannot do inter-round communications like other panel studies. Instead, they devote a large part of the data collection effort to pre-field locating efforts in which they email, mail, and call sample members to alert them of the upcoming study with the goal of learning where they are, updating contact information, and approaching them about the study that will begin in a few months. An additional level of effort individually searches for panel members using property searches and Accurint. They are also seeking IRB permission to reach out to sample members via social media on Facebook, as well as reaching out to alumni organizations to see if they are willing to let people in those graduating classes know that they may be asked to participate in a study done by NORC at the University of Chicago.

Canas said multiple modes of response for HS&B FU are offered: telephone, a web survey, or a paper survey. According to Canas, everyone starts with an assignment to a singular mode and then switches modes about halfway through the data collection; the opportunity to do a last-chance paper survey is offered at the end of data collection. She explained this ensures that they are targeting people in modes that they would prefer and enjoy participating in using the mode respondents used previously.

Canas also described the mix of pre- and post-incentives to gain participation for both the survey portion as well as new biomarker components. These two parts are treated separately so panel members receive an incentive for participating in the survey and then an incentive for participating in the biomarker data collection. Through an adaptive design, differential incentives are provided for people who are likely to participate based on past rounds and other characteristics, such as those Grodsky had noted were related to panel attrition. They are about to launch some increased incentive packages.

Because HS&B panel members have never participated in a biomarker data collection in this study before, a number of different efforts will be made to get people interested, agree to consent, and participate in biomarker data collection this round. Based on a pretest, they reframed the blood draw to a health visit, which includes a blood draw plus some health measures and a saliva sample. Reframing it in this way made people a little more interested, she reported. The web survey included a video in which one of the PIs, Jennifer Manly, talked about the importance of the health visit. This was done to put a face to the research and emphasize its importance to address lower rates of consent on the web.

Canas concluded by noting that refusal conversion efforts have helped increase the consent rates and interest in the biomarker aspect of the study. If panel members say they are not interested at the first contact, a field interviewer team calls them back and lets them know about the health portion, answers questions, and provides an increased incentive.

Retention in Longitudinal Studies of Aging

Pamela Herd is a professor in the McCourt School of Public Policy at Georgetown University and a PI of the Wisconsin Longitudinal Study (2010–present). She described the Wisconsin Longitudinal Study (WLS), which has been tracking about one out of every three Wisconsin high school graduates from the class of 1957. Siblings were added starting in the 1970s and more fully in the early 1990s. The study participants are currently in their early 80s, so Herd emphasized that she is talking about retention in a life course longitudinal panel, especially for much older samples.

Herd noted that WLS response rates over time have been about 80 to 90 percent, with higher response rates among the primary graduates and slightly lower response rates among the siblings. The primary sample basically had a 100 percent response rate at baseline, so they have information on everyone in the sample frame. Roughly two-thirds of their living sample are still involved in the project.

Herd said that the data collected cover basically every aspect of the panel participants' lives, and biological data added over time include saliva samples and data on the microbiome, as well as administrative data like Social Security earnings and Medicare data. Herd said that some of this information has been important for retention, as it helps the researchers track participants over time. She also noted that engagement over the years has fostered participants' sense of involvement in the project.

Herd described a new study, the WLS dementia project. They have two waves of data collection over a 5-year period, and each wave includes a preliminary half-hour phone survey. They conduct a follow-up in-person survey with people who they believe are at risk for dementia. Because of COVID-19, the in-home survey has temporarily been converted to the telephone. She noted that although there is a lot of interest in assessing cognitive change and cognitive outcomes, it does add to the burden on study participants. The team is figuring out how to minimize the burden and keep participants engaged when some of what the study participants are doing may be more challenging for them.

Herd described the characteristics of participants at higher risk of dropping out of the study, such as lower educational attainment. Similar to the HS&B FU described by Grodsky and Canas, the WLS has a measure of adolescent cognitive functioning, and it is a strong predictor of attrition over time, with those who have lower cognitive functioning more likely to drop out. This has implications for studying dementia and cognitive change in later life, Herd said, but having baseline data can help adjust for nonresponse bias.

Herd also highlighted the challenges of doing phone interviews and trying to assess cognition and hearing decline much later in life, because by the time people are in their 70s and early 80s, these conditions are fairly prevalent. In-person surveys are needed, and even they are challenging. Poorer health and hearing issues were related to higher attrition from the study. Another challenge Herd noted was that with older samples, some respondents have different residences in the summer and winter. She said this affects high-SES rather than low-SES participants, but it is more difficult to keep track of them because they move.

Herd also described an example of how they subsample for different projects within the broader sample and the implications of nonresponse. She noted that in the microbiome study, they found differences between respondents and nonrespondents within the subsample. She also said it is important to pay attention to this because the kinds of weighting adjustments that one might do are trickier with a small sample.

WLS researchers take a number of steps to retain participants. Herd stressed the importance of repeated contacts both to figure out where participants are living and to keep some kind of engagement or connection between them and the project. The materials communicate clearly to participants and provide meaningful engagement about what are they contributing to the research, giving them a connection with the project and what the researchers are learning from them. She said this matters for long-term panel engagement. She added that data on participants specifically geared toward figuring out where they will be for the next round is very important because people move. Older adults may not move for work, but they often move in with their children or into environments with more caregiving support. She also said that the quality of the interviewers matters in terms of effectively getting people to keep participating and engaged.

Herd emphasized that although response rates matter, it is selective attrition that is of concern, so they do targeted nonresponse follow-up among subsamples to reduce bias or better model to account for attrition. Targeted doorstep visits are effective when other modes have failed. More burdensome kinds of interviews make it harder to get people to engage again because they expect another long interview. Thus, they are very careful about minimizing burden.

Herd shared examples of materials sent to participants and noted some participants contact them and request more information. Although they do not have explicit data, they receive feedback from participants that they feel loyalty toward the project the longer they have been involved in it, which matters for their continued participation. Similarly linked is a sense of belonging to something bigger than themselves and the feeling of making a contribution to the greater good. Herd said it would be useful to explore survey experiments to see how much these feelings matter for studies like WLS, HS&B FU, and others.

Herd concluded by describing challenges going forward. In terms of managing attrition and nonresponse in lifelong panel studies, she referred to two approaches already discussed in the workshop. The first is trying to keep people in, but she stressed the importance of drawing on administrative data to fill in when they lose track of people. The other approach is developing modeling techniques around selection to deal with nonresponse. She noted that longitudinal studies have extensive data on people who were lost due to mortality or attrition, and leveraging those modeling techniques to adjust for bias is worth continued work.

Discussion

Davern started the discussion period by asking the presenters what they saw as the most important emerging ways of engaging and retaining respondents over the last 4 or 5 years. As a follow-up, he asked what strategy did they consider likely to be the most important over the next 2 to 5 years.

Herd acknowledged the tradeoff between cost versus retention and response, and the high costs while maintaining sample quality. In her view, one of the most critical things is keeping some element of in-person recruitment, whether that is shifting toward in-person interviewing for people who cannot be reached through other modes, or very selective targeting of in-person efforts to manage nonresponse bias. She said the continued use of in-person data collection is critical, but needs to be targeted given how expensive it is.

Canas noted from a lower-cost perspective, email and texting in panel studies have proven to be reasonably effective. HS&B FU has a web survey, and emails have provided the biggest bump in completing those web surveys, in addition to texting. Grodsky concurred with Herd about the need to maintain contact and develop identity and rapport with sample members. He noted a challenge between funding cycles is the lack of a built-in mechanism for sending out birthday cards, newsletters, and occasional communications, which are not terribly expensive but could yield substantial rewards back in the field in terms of the representativeness of the sample and response rates.

Watson agreed and suggested building rapport with respondents, showing them how relevant their stories are, and feeding back some of the results, all of which are becoming more important.

John Phillips returned to comments made by Herd and Carol Ryff (see Chapter 2) regarding loyalty or trust. He asked whether pamphlets about what the study is finding or other updates on the studies build trust. He questioned whether these efforts could have an impact on things like willingness to consent for a biomarker, apart from the loyalty built from being in the panel for a long time. He noted that HRS began doing biomarker collection after participants had already been in the study for quite a while, which may have a meaningful effect on trust just by itself. He asked the presenters for their thoughts on trust and the ways to build trust in a study to not only maintain a panel, but also to improve initial response rates.

Ryff responded that she would frame the issue more in terms of rapport than trust, because trust implies more complex interactions. She suggested they could study participants' responses to the newsletters more systematically and what they think they are getting out of them. She noted that her study's newsletters are very high quality, with a science journalist distilling the research information into engaging and readable four-page brochures. She was unclear whether the newsletters cultivate loyalty, but they do give the participants a sense that they are contributing to important science, which she said is a huge hook. However, Ryff said she does not favor distributing the newsletters to some people but not others to test effectiveness. She noted that giving back the science is an important part of taxpayer-funded research, and is also part of research translation. For that reason, she added, the MIDUS newsletters are posted on the study website.

David Weir commented that MIDUS has great results and produces excellent reports; however, other studies may not have the resources or breadth of interesting results to share. He has observed that HRS participants want information that will make them healthier. He suggested different studies could collaborate to generalize findings so that they can provide research on health, not necessarily tied to a specific study. He noted that while participants like to see that they are contributing directly, they also could be getting something back from the experts conducting the study. Herd countered that one challenge to this idea, which Grodsky noted earlier, is panel-conditioning effects. When her study sends out findings, she noted, they are thinking carefully about what they are conveying and how they are conveying it. She called for more research to understand exactly what participants want. She noted that conversations with participants in their microbiome study completely changed the strategy for how and what was communicated to them. Davern concluded the session by noting the importance of listening to the respondents to increase retention.

PARTICIPANT ENGAGEMENT: INSIGHTS FROM BEHAVIORAL SCIENCE RESEARCH

Recruitment and Consent of Vulnerable Populations

Bettina Drake is a professor of surgery at Washington University School of Medicine in the Division of Public Health Sciences and the associate director of Community Outreach and Engagement at the Siteman Cancer Center. She is a cancer epidemiologist and health disparities researcher with expertise in community-based research. She began by noting that diversity in research participation is needed in order to conduct the most valuable research possible and that includes diversity by race, rural/urban status, and geographies, as well as individuals who have regular access to care and those who live in medically underserved areas. The reason, she continued, is to obtain generalizable results so that interventions and treatments can have the biggest impact in communities and patient populations, but also address disparities across race, ethnicity, and socioeconomic status.

Drake described studies focused on recruitment to biorepositories, but underscored these strategies apply broadly. She noted that consent for the secondary use of biospecimens is both a critical ethical issue and a policy issue. Patients are rightly concerned about how long the samples will be stored and what research is going to be conducted. She said that the literature provides little empirical evidence for donors' preferences or different models of informed consent.

The first study Drake described was to understand barriers and strategies to improve participation in biorepositories for African American men, specifically for recruiting a prostate cancer cohort. Recruitment was made at the time of diagnosis with consent to grant access to their medical records, completion of a questionnaire, and collection of biospecimens. The biospecimen was collected at the time of treatment, and it was a consent to allow the specimens that were already being removed or blood draws that were already happening to have additional tubes of blood drawn to allow those specimens to be included in a biorepository. Initially they had very low minority participation. She said that about 70 African American men were included in focus groups, about half of whom were prostate cancer survivors.

Drake shared some of the themes and quotes that came out of the focus groups identifying strategies to increase participation. Participants suggested not recruiting at the doctor's office because patients might be in pain or thinking about other things. The focus groups suggested talking about participation to people at younger ages so that when they end up in a health care setting, it is not completely new information. Mistrust and privacy were key themes that emerged, and some people were concerned their specimens would be taken and used for personal gain. Henrietta Lacks was brought up in a couple of the focus groups, Drake reported.

Drake said that another theme was that education about what the biorepository is and what the researchers were trying to do was important. Some participants said that anything that can further research that can help their family members was important, while others commented that as long as there is not a lot of pain involved in the procedures, they would be willing to participate. Physician endorsement of the study was helpful to address the lack of trust in research.

According to Drake, this information led to changes in the recruitment strategy for the prostate cancer cohort. They provided information to all of the physicians about this study, and gave them fliers to put in their waiting rooms as well as little cards for participants to take with them. She said that one of the more important but also time-consuming strategies was to include an additional approach for each participant. The first attempt to recruit participants was between diagnosis and treatment, which is a small window. Prior to this time period, they would have an informational meeting where the study was introduced as an opportunity, and patients were told that their urologist or medical oncologist was aware of it, and they were encouraged to talk with their doctors about the study. The study team then offered to call the patients or meet them at their next appointment. She said this offer increased the comfort and the trust among many participants and increased the percentage of minorities by 7 to 12 percentage points over a couple of years, and that percentage is even higher now.

The next study that Drake described was designed to assess the impact of different consent models on intentions to participate in a biorepository for secondary research among a diverse sample of women. Four models of consent were used: (1) study-specific consent is when researchers ask a participant's permission before each future study in which they would use their sample; (2) broad consent is when researchers only ask for the participant's permission once for all future studies; (3) the opt-out option is when researchers inform the participant that their sample may be used for future studies, unless the participant directs them not to store the sample for future use; and (4) notice is when researchers tell participants that if they participate in this study, their sample will be used for future studies, without giving the participant an option to say yes or no.

Drake discussed the qualitative work done with a sample of 60 diverse women, of whom about half were African American and half were Caucasian. The women were asked to identify their most and least preferred options. They found that broad consent was the most preferred and that notice was the least preferred model of consent. Study-specific consent was the second most preferred and the second least preferred method of consent.

Drake shared qualitative comments that reflected the participants' reactions to each of the consent models. The notice model was perceived to have the benefits of being simple, efficient, and requiring little effort by the participant. However, concerns about the notice model were a loss of control over their sample, insufficient information, and it was discourteous not to ask for permission to use the samples. For the broad consent model, some of the benefits were that it was a good balance of the different model options, providing more control over the patient's sample and less burden on the researchers. A few concerns raised regarding the broad consent model related to insufficient information about each individual future study. The study-specific model was perceived to provide information about all future studies and give the patient more control over their samples. Participants also raised concerns that it could slow down the research, and is more trouble for both the participant and the researcher.

Drake then described an experiment to assess the intent to participate after being presented a randomly selected consent model of three options: notice, broad, and study specific. The sample consisted of 357 women, of whom 56 were African American, about one-third had a high school degree or below, about one-third had a college degree or above, and about one-quarter had a limited health literacy level. Drake said that trust in medical research was a consistent and significant predictor of intention to donate for each of these consent models.

Although they did not observe any racial differences in intent to donate for any of the three consent models, Black participants reported wanting more control overall than White participants of their samples, Drake said. Individuals who participated in medical research in the past were comfortable with less control of their samples than those who had not participated in medical research. She noted an interaction between race and trust in research and doctors, such that trust in medical research, as well as trust in doctors, was significantly and negatively associated with the level of control, but only among White participants, not Black participants.

Drake summarized her research among men, particularly African American men, and a diverse sample of women as illustrative of how to better educate and work with patients and community members on consent models for biorepositories. She said that these lessons can be applied for other types of research as well.

Harnessing New Communication Methods to Support Survey Research in the 21st Century

Amelia Burke-Garcia is a health communications professional focusing on digital outreach strategies at NORC at the University of Chicago. She is also the author of the book *Influencing Health, A Comprehensive*

Guide to Working with Online Influencers. Burke-Garcia focused her talk on how digital and social media can be used throughout the survey lifespan to help with some of the challenges that the survey research field is facing, particularly related to engagement. Burke-Garcia noted that the survey and polling business has been in crisis with response rates falling for more than 30 years, and high-quality face-to-face surveys now rarely reach a 70 percent response rate.

According to Burke-Garcia, this trend is driven by a number of factors, which taken together make the whole world harder to survey. She pointed to displacement of people both within the United States as well as globally, explaining displaced persons are not necessarily living in their homelands and may or may not be counted as part of the populations being surveyed. She also noted that many Americans have direct access to the internet via mobile devices only; research has shown that with so much information coming every day, people tend to lose their concentration after just 8 seconds; and trust is waning, with just 18 percent of Americans saying that they can trust the government.

Burke-Garcia said these factors have implications for doing survey research because the devices and the technology that people use are critically important for how they access information, as well as participate in web-based surveys. She urged thoughtfulness in terms of engaging participants, and carefully considering the length of the questionnaire that respondents are asked complete. At least pre-COVID-19, people were spending more time in the workplace than at home, which makes it harder to contact and survey people at their homes, a key mode of data collection for many surveys.

Burke-Garcia also described developments with new types of data being made available, new ways of communicating with people, reaching people, and identifying them, which constitute a paradigm shift for survey research that uses multiple data sources, multiple modes, and multiple frames. For example, there are more than 3 million Google searches every minute; more than 300 million monthly active Amazon users globally; more than 2 billion monthly active Apple device users globally; and more than 2.2 billion people on Facebook globally.

Burke-Garcia advocated using new and emerging communication channels to support and amplify survey research, and broadening the conceptualization of what social and digital media mean for survey research. Burke-Garcia said that it is not just about the message, text, or images used to communicate, but that these platforms, these data, and the people that use them offer some additional context. Her focus is on how to use social and digital media throughout the survey life cycle, including sampling, identifying, reaching, persuading, and interviewing respondents.

In terms of sampling people, Burke-Garcia said that social media offers opportunities for leveraging and building on venue-based time-space sampling. People congregate as groups and get together for virtual events on Facebook, but those events differ from in-person real-time events where some kind of survey data collection might take place. However, she said that leveraging groups that come together around similar issues or topics can be effective to get additional types of samples and subgroups to participate in research. In addition, she pointed to online groups and online influencer networks that offer opportunities to potentially do some additional sampling work.

In seeking to identify people, Burke-Garcia said work is being done that looks at how to leverage different variables shared through social media to both deepen an understanding of survey responses and supplement gaps in data collection. She cautioned about risks in terms of what data people make available and the accuracy, but suggested researchers could passively collect some data to reduce burden on respondents.

Burke-Garcia described ways to reach and engage people in social media to participate. One main way is to leverage paid social media advertising to promote surveys to people who may not otherwise know about them. Thinking about surveys as brands can improve understanding about how to message why data are being collected and what value these data will have in their lives or communities, she said, adding that the messaging also can help garner trust to participate. Paid social media ads are fairly easy to develop, launch, and manage, she commented. She noted that one can see fairly quickly what messages may or may not work well, which improves efficiency in trying to reach and engage people to participate.

Burke-Garcia also noted work to use social media as an additional contact channel for follow up to lower attrition. She suggested thinking about people's social networks as additional opportunities to connect with them over time, as their address or phone often may change, especially for harder-to-reach populations. She said that their social media does not change as frequently, which provides another venue for contacting and tracing.

For persuading people, Burke-Garcia said social media advertising can also be very effective. She encouraged running ads in an A/B testing approach, which reveals which messages are more persuasive versus those that are less persuasive based on people's engagement with the ads, how they click through to a survey, if they start a survey, and if they are eligible to complete it. In addition, online and social media influencers can be very persuasive and powerful in raising public awareness about the survey and establishing legitimacy of the research. She added that hearing about the survey from a friend can be quite persuasive because that person is a trusted voice.

In terms of interviewing people, Burke-Garcia noted the potential for passively collecting what people are doing and accessing some of their data can be highly valuable to deepen an understanding of what is collected in the survey. She also noted opportunities for active data collection by soliciting feedback from particular groups in social or in digital media as a way to crowdsource information and get feedback perhaps less formally than a survey, but still add value.

Challenges exist with these approaches, which are in various stages of testing and implementation, Burke-Garcia cautioned. Social media platforms and the way people use them are changing rapidly, but many types of groups, especially harder-to-reach groups, congregate within different online communities. She encouraged experimenting with and exploring how to use social media to augment traditional survey methods. Ad blockers, inactive users, fake accounts, and bots pose additional challenges, and she urged having an understanding and awareness of users.

Transparency, privacy, consent, and appropriate use of the data apply to these data as they do to survey data, Burke-Garcia stressed. Tools for analyzing these data are improving but more work is needed to better understand respondents' sentiments. Other considerations she briefly noted were the available budgets, threats to the validity of the study from human error and misrepresentation, and the risk for a Hawthorne effect by participating and engaging within these communities. Burke-Garcia urged considering these challenges to ensure that research is implemented correctly.

Burke-Garcia concluded by pointing toward future directions and the work that needs to be done, urging investments in pilot and feasibility studies to test if and how these approaches work and to identify weaknesses and gaps. She said that new frameworks need to be explored to integrate these different types of data with traditional survey research. She also noted that work is needed on error structures for these new data sources, and developing protocols for appropriately and successfully using social media data. She underscored the opportunity to reach new populations, suggesting that engaging people in different ways can hopefully create more engagement and participation in survey research into the future.

Discussion

John Phillips kicked off a discussion about using social media to provide awareness, comfort, or trust in participating in a survey, and he asked who the influencers are for aging studies. Burke-Garcia replied a large majority of online influencer spaces are comprised of moms and dads who become caretakers of their children and their aging parents. She suggested an opportunity to engage them to help bring the message home to their peers who may then influence their parents to participate. She added that older adult influencers tend to be heavy Facebook users and may participate in groups for social community or to look at photos and stay in touch with their families.

Phillips also referred to a comment by Drake that suggests a theme running through several presentations: When people have some experience with the research enterprise, they tend to be a lot more comfortable with it. He said he is thinking about ways to use this observation to further scientific engagement for the community and to improve people's willingness to participate and consent to research. He noted the opportunity in longitudinal studies to build that trust over time, but the initial ask to participate is in some respect the most important point.

Drake responded that trust is very important, but so is "pulling back the curtain" and helping people understand what is going on behind the scenes. She underscored the opportunity to educate and engage community members before they get to a point where they are being asked to participate in a study or a clinical trial. Drake said researchers often mistakenly take for granted that participants understand what is done with their specimens and data and why. Helping them understand that ahead of time can be important in gaining their trust and participation.

Phillips concluded by noting an interesting potential link between the two presentations in this session. He suggested bringing the experience with research that Drake described to a broader population through the types of social media that Burke-Garcia discussed, perhaps through testimonials to make people more comfortable with a study.

4

Informed Consent

This chapter summarizes the presentations and discussion in two sessions on September 28 that focused on informed consent. Vetta Sanders Thompson chaired both sessions, the first on the complexity of informed consent, and the second on ethical considerations for obtaining informed consent. Questions and discussion for both sessions followed the end of the second session.

THE COMPLEXITY OF INFORMED CONSENT

Understanding Consent to Data Linkage

Annette Jäckle is professor for survey methodology at the Institute for Social and Economic Research at the University of Essex and associate director for innovations for Understanding Society. Jäckle explained this study, Understanding Society, is a longitudinal household panel and the UK equivalent to the Panel Study of Income Dynamics. Data are collected using a combination of web, face-to-face, and telephone interviewing, and they request respondents' consent to link data to different government administrative records and financial data. A study observation is that respondents who complete the survey online are much less likely to consent to linkages than when they complete the survey with a face-to-face interviewer, and the gap is 30 percentage points. Jäckle said they are trying to solve this problem and increase informed consent by web respondents.

Jäckle briefly reviewed the key findings from the survey methods research literature on data linkage consent. She pointed to the variation in consent rates depending on the topic, with consent rates to link financial data tending to be lower than to link health or education data. There are also differences in consent rates between interviewers, and very little consistency in the predictors of who consents between studies, within studies over time, or within studies for different consents. A surprising number of experimental studies have tried different ways of asking the consent question and have not been very successful at increasing consent, she commented. Her conclusion is that consent decisions can be influenced, but it is not yet known how. Several studies have shown that many respondents do not fully understand the request for consent to data linkage, which suggests an opportunity to improve understanding.

Both the Understanding Society and the Health and Retirement Study have documented that when asking people who did not give consent in one wave if they will consent in a later wave, half of the nonconsenters provide consent the next time they are asked, she reported. She said that this finding suggests it is not a fixed decision and can potentially be influenced. Research looking at multiple consents asked in one interview appeared to show a latent willingness to consent, she continued, but this willingness to consent does not seem to hold over time. It does not seem to be a stable characteristic, which suggests situational factors are important. She concluded that the research question is how respondents make the decision whether or not to consent.

Jäckle described her group's research project to examine how respondents decide whether to consent or not and why respondents are less likely to consent when they are completing the survey online than with a face-to-face interviewer. The project started with qualitative, in-depth interviews, drawing participants from a separate Innovation Panel, which is a sample of 1,500 households that are interviewed in the same manner as the main sample. She explained the findings from these qualitative interviews were used to develop a conceptual framework about how people make the consent decision, generate hypotheses, and then experimentally test some of the hypotheses using both the Innovation Panel and an additional online access panel to increase their sample size.

As Jäckle discussed, their conceptual framework for consent draws upon the cognitive model of the survey response process, which states that in order to answer a survey question, respondents have to understand the question, retrieve relevant information from memory, form a judgment, and then decide what they are actually going to say; however, respondents do not necessarily execute this process optimally. The study drew upon the rational versus heuristic decision-making literature or System 1 versus System 2 processing, which has shown that people make the bulk of their decisions using System 1 processing, which means they are making quick, top-of-the-head decisions, but that they can also override those quick decisions and make much more effortful, deliberate decisions. They also drew upon the literature in psychology about how people make decisions in real life, noting that people reduce the amount of information that they use to base their decision on.

Jäckle described the conceptual framework for how respondents decide to consent (Figure 4-1). The green box on the right-hand side contains the outcomes of interest: whether the participant provides consent, how well they understand the request, and how confident they are in their consent decision. The red box on the left includes the characteristics of each respondent, their prior experiences and knowledge, their cognitive capacity, and their attitudes and behaviors. In addition, she noted that the trust the respondents have in the organizations involved and the survey team may affect the decision. For example, some government departments may be perceived as more trusted than others. She noted that elements of the survey design, such as the content and the format of the consent request, and the mode for the request are also relevant. These factors might have direct influences on the outcomes, she suggested.

Jäckle said that the blue box in the middle of Figure 4-1 represents what goes on in the respondents' minds, and how they are making this decision, which is the focus of the study. The study assumes a continuum of decision processes, with some respondents making the decision in a more reflective way and others in a less reflective way. She noted that respondents are not directly observed in this decision process, but are asked to self-report how they made the decision. They also measure other indicators. For

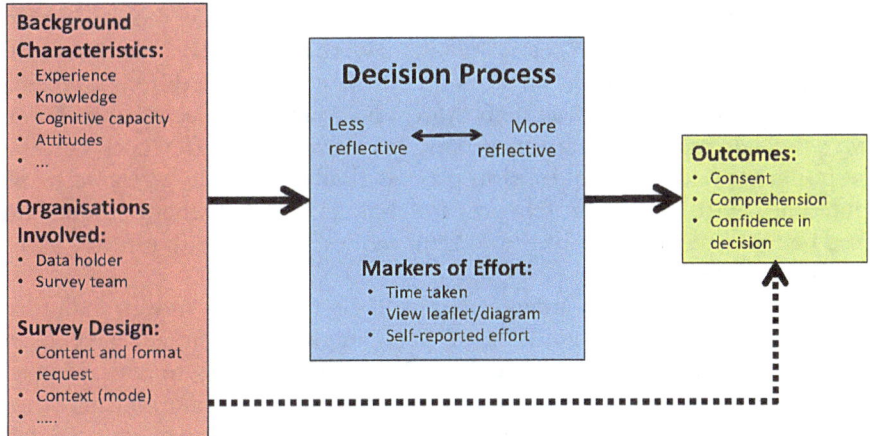

FIGURE 4-1 How respondents decide whether to consent.
SOURCE: Annette Jäckle workshop presentation, September 28, 2021, and Burton et al. (2021).

example, they look at how long people take to answer the consent question, which should vary depending on whether the respondent is making more rather than less reflective decisions. They can look at whether respondents are reading additional information, and ask them to self-report how much effort they consider that they put into answering the consent question.

The focus of the study was on a single consent question about linking tax records, which asked if the participant gave permission for the researchers to pass their name, address, sex, and date of birth to Her Majesty's Revenue and Customs for the purpose of linking their tax records to their survey responses. Participants were not asked for their unique national identity insurance number, but they were asked background and follow-up questions about how they made this decision. Jäckle noted that they replicated this research design in several samples, including the Innovation Panel and an online access panel, and included both web and face-to-face respondents.

Participants had several options to indicate how they made their decision to consent, Jäckle reported. Just over one-third said that they made a reflective decision on whether or not to consent. They based their decision on thinking about the consequences of what would happen if they consented or on thinking about how much they trust the organizations involved. The rest predominantly used heuristic decision processes, for example basing their decision on gut feeling or habit, and were simplifying the decision and basing it on just some aspects rather than all the information available.

Jäckle described additional indicators to validate the self-reported measure of how respondents said they made their decision. Respondents who were less reflective and made decisions based on habit or gut feeling spent less time answering the question than those who made more reflective decisions. More reflective decision makers were more likely to look at additional information, and they also said that they used more different types of information in their decision than those who were less reflective. Jäckle said that the self-reported decision process measures real differences between respondents and that the decision process that people use is related to the outcomes, with more reflective decision makers having higher consent rates and better understanding of the consent request; however, that is not necessarily a causal effect.

In terms of why respondents are less likely to consent in web than face-to-face encounters, Jäckle said the 30-percentage-point difference in consent rates between modes is causal: Respondents are less likely to consent when they answer online than face-to-face, and they also understand the request less well. Respondents online are more concerned about privacy and data security, and they answer the consent questions less thoroughly, more quickly, and are less likely to read additional information than those in person. Online respondents are more likely to make habit-based decisions and less likely to make reflective decisions than those in person, she added. She pointed out that the interviewers are not providing additional information or reassurance.

In conclusion, Jäckle said that there are clear differences in how people make the consent decision. The majority of respondents do not use a reflective process, are unlikely to read additional information, and make the decision very quickly. Just providing more information is unlikely to increase informed consent, she said, but the researchers do not know how they can get more people to make a reflective decision and whether it is possible to shift people's decision-making style and thereby increase informed consent.

Biomeasures: Gaining Cooperation and Informed Consent

Katie O'Doherty is senior research director in the Health Sciences Department at NORC at the University of Chicago. O'Doherty focused on gaining cooperation and informed consent for a variety of different biomeasures across several different projects. These measures included sensory measurements, body measurements, performance of physical activities, and biosamples, such as blood and urine.

O'Doherty first described gaining cooperation and consent in interviewer-administered studies. Advance materials are provided with high-level information about biomeasure collection, but not extensive detail. Next, a field interviewer provides additional information at the doorstep to gain cooperation for the interview. Once the interviewer gains cooperation, they do a written informed consent for the interview, which includes an overview of the biomeasures, the risks, the benefits, the results, and confidentiality. Interviewers answer the respondents' questions and address any concerns. The interviewers tell respondents that they can still participate in an interview even if they are unsure about a biomeasure, and that the interviewer will explain it in detail at the appropriate point.

The biomeasure collection takes place in the middle of the interview, O'Doherty said, which allows the interviewer to establish rapport and gain some trust with the respondent before asking for these measures. Verbal consent is obtained for the individual measures and the interviewer provides detailed explanation of these measures at the time of collection. Respondents receive a single incentive for the interview, including the questionnaire and biomeasures, rather than separate incentives, and the researchers try to share results from these measures with respondents. O'Doherty said that pretesting was helpful to make the process go more smoothly, and to address respondent questions and concerns.

O'Doherty shared biomeasure cooperation rates from the National Social Life, Health and Aging Project (NSHAP) from three in-person rounds of data collection (Table 4-1). The rates shown in the table are the

TABLE 4-1 NSHAP In-Person Biomeasure Cooperation Rates

Biomeasure	Round 1	Round 2	Round 3
Weight	98%	98%	98%
Waist	97%	98%	97%
Height	99%	98%	99%
BP and Pulse	98%	98%	98%
Balance	—	—	99%
Timed Walk	—	96%	98%
Chair Stands	—	94%	98%
Smell	98%	96%	96%
Saliva	89%	95%	91%
Vaginal Swabs	68%	73%	—
Blood Spots	85%	92%	92%
Accelerometry	—	78%	84%

SOURCE: Adapted from Katie O'Doherty workshop presentation, September 28, 2021.

percentage of respondents who agreed to the measure out of the number asked in the interview. Many of the measures have very high cooperation rates, but rates are a little lower for saliva and blood spots, and are the lowest for vaginal swabs and accelerometry, which involves wearing a device for 8 days.

O'Doherty next described self-administered biomeasure collection. She began by showing a picture of the NSHAP BioBox (Figure 4-2), which was developed for remote data collection in Round 4 of the study. The box contains a BioBooklet with a yellow cover, which has the step-by-step instructions that respondents would follow to collect their own health measures. The supply box includes all the supplies needed to collect these measures and a place for specimen storage. O'Doherty noted that they simplified the collection instructions greatly for respondents. Field interviewers helped organize the supplies and the presentation of the instructions, and a lab pilot and two pretests of the BioBox were conducted. She said that they will not obtain all of the same biomeasures collected during in-person interviews, because the BioBox does not contain blood pressure monitors or scales.

Round 4 remote data collection is currently in the field, O'Doherty said. Advanced materials are sent first, with an invitation letter that contains high-level information about the questionnaire and the BioBox, along with a brochure. Participants can complete the questionnaire by web, phone, or paper and pencil, which are offered sequentially as options.

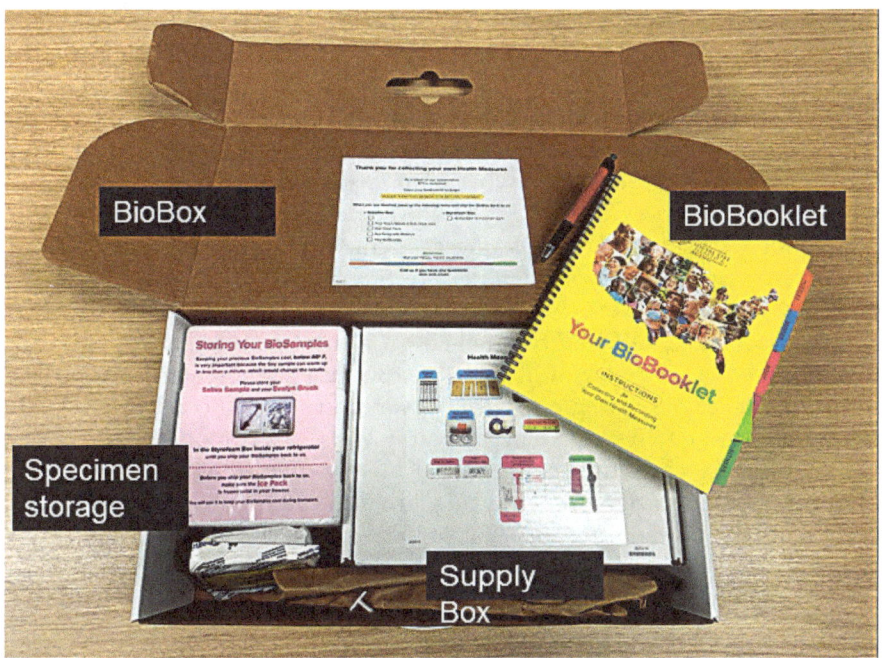

FIGURE 4-2 NSHAP BioBox for remote collection in Round 4.
SOURCE: Katie O'Doherty workshop presentation, September 28, 2021.

Regardless of mode, the questionnaire ends with an invitation to participate in the BioBox. To gain cooperation, the information provides an overview of why participation is important, what they are being asked to do, what measures would be collected, how long it would take, and the incentive that they would receive, which an interviewer would normally explain for gaining cooperation. People who are interested then receive much more detailed additional consent language, which includes the risks and benefits and how their data will be protected. If they consent to receive the BioBox, it is mailed to them along with a copy of their consent form and a prepaid incentive.

O'Doherty shared results from a pretest conducted last year that involved comparing six different BioBox types to assess consent with each approach. Three different types of boxes varied by what measures were included and the length of time required to do them, with two taking about an hour and another about an hour and a half. Three included collecting blood, and three did not. Not asking for blood yielded slightly higher return rates than asking for blood, and the boxes that took less time for respondents to complete also had slightly higher return rates than the boxes that took longer. Based on these results, O'Doherty related, they decided to go with a one-hour box for Round 4 and to collect blood because of its importance to the study aims.

O'Doherty briefly described the health visits with a phlebotomist in the High School and Beyond (HS&B) study, which Eric Grodsky and Rachel Canas discussed earlier in the workshop (see Chapter 3). The procedures were similar to those for the NSHAP BioBox, she pointed out. In addition, a web video was created to try to increase consent because a pretest showed that web consent was lower than phone consent. As this study is still in the field, results are not available to share.

In conclusion, O'Doherty touched on refusal conversion for both the NSHAP BioBox and HS&B health visit. Because gaining cooperation and informed consent are attempted without an in-person interviewer to explain things in more detail, experienced interviewers call respondents to revisit the biomeasure collection consent and answer questions about a month after a remote interview. She said they are also offering a higher incentive, and preliminary results are showing success in converting some biomeasure nonrespondents.

The Complexity of Informed Consent

Christine Grady is a nurse, bioethicist, and senior investigator and chief of the Department of Bioethics at the National Institutes of Health Clinical Center. Grady spoke in general terms about the complexity of informed consent, drawing upon her research and experience as well as the literature. She first described the components of informed consent: Consent for people who have the capacity involves giving them study information in a relevant way, determining that they can understand the information and can use it to make a voluntary choice about whether or not to participate, and then authorizing participation in some way. She acknowledged the process is much harder than it theoretically sounds like it should be.

Informed consent is complex because of enduring challenges in making decisions about disclosure and understanding voluntary choice, she continued. It is also complicated by differences in individuals' motivations and expectations, their capacity to understand and to make decisions, their tolerance for and perception of inconvenience and burden, their trust, and their responses to incentives.

With respect to disclosure of information, Grady opined the hardest decision to make is what information should be disclosed in a way that is accessible, relevant, and understandable to participants. She stressed the importance of how the information is presented, whether it is on the web or in person, beyond its amount and complexity. Not enough is known about how different groups accept different presentations of information, but acceptance probably varies by age, socioeconomic circumstances, and culture. Considerations in terms of how information should be presented for the purposes of consent depend on the setting and the population. For example, presenting information about treatment to a very sick patient in the intensive care unit with COVID-19 is very different than presenting information to somebody in the outpatient setting for a blood sample.

In terms of understanding information, Grady referred to a meta-analysis that looked at how well people understand information about participation in research and found that it is not very good.[1] Specifically, no particular part of the study information was understood by more than 75 percent of the people. Some key features of studies like placebo use and randomization are understood by 50 percent or less, which means that one in every two people who are participating in a placebo-controlled study do not really understand what that means. Grady said that a number of factors affect understanding, including age, education, and features like pain, cognitive impairment, and literacy, as well as expectations and familiarity. She noted that a large percentage of research participants in cancer clinical trials say they trust their providers and do not need to pay attention to the details of the study or the benefits and risks.

In her research on understanding and consent, Grady reported a fairly large percentage of people in surveys admit that they do not really read the information provided to them. A number of studies have tried to show that changing the length of a consent form or adding videos or other enhancements to the consent process may improve understanding, but the results show that no one approach, other than person-to-person discussion, seems to consistently increase understanding in the process of informed consent. Less is known about what information people really want. Although people say they are satisfied with the information received, asking them specific questions shows the limits to their understanding. Perhaps, she suggested, people do not want or feel they need some of the information that researchers think is necessary.

Grady discussed several implications of understanding and consent for longitudinal studies. Some evidence suggests that people forget information that was provided to them at an earlier point in time, she said. When asked at a later point in time what they remember, they remember much less, and say that they want more information, especially about things that they have determined over time have become meaningful to them. Questions remain about the right way to ensure that people are consenting over time, noting some studies might call for a legitimate reason to reconsent people. Other models, such as dynamic consent, sometimes used for biobanks, give participants a fair amount of control over how much they are sharing in a

---

[1] See https://www.who.int/bulletin/volumes/93/3/14-141390.pdf.

specific time, and they can pull their data or decide to be in one study but not another.

Consent understanding is complicated because science is complicated, Grady commented, and trying to explain to people what researchers are doing and why is challenging because health literacy and science literacy in general are quite low. A constant debate in the bioethics world centers on how much participants should understand in order to give consent, she related. Most people believe it depends on the kind of study; as risks or novelty increase, then maybe the threshold of understanding should be higher, but there are also different kinds of misunderstanding, some of which are probably more problematic ethically than others.

Turning to the next component of informed consent, voluntary decision about participating or continuing to participate, Grady explained this involves whether people feel like they can say no, whether they feel any pressure, and if so, from whom. Family and friends may apply pressure, but it could also come from the research team or a doctor. She said that some bioethicists think incentives place pressure on people, but others disagree.

Research examining why people continue to participate in longitudinal studies has identified three primary reasons, Grady reported. The most important reason is perceived benefit, that people either find medical benefit in terms of access to an experimental intervention, personal benefit like money or attention, or feeling good about what they are doing. The second reason is people feel good about making contributions to science and to others. The third is that many people say that they want to continue their commitment to the study. She noted that studies where people are asked if they were willing to participate in different kinds of studies have a similar pattern of findings: high levels of willingness, with decreased willingness when there is more risk or invasiveness, or when more time or burden is involved. She concluded by calling for a better understanding about why people want or do not want to participate in longitudinal studies, how to make them as convenient and low burden as possible, how to earn trust, and how incentives play a role.

ETHICAL CONSIDERATIONS FOR OBTAINING INFORMED CONSENT

Vetta Sanders Thompson commented that Grady's presentation provides a good transition to a discussion of ethical issues encountered in longitudinal study consent, particularly variability over time and what participants are asked to consent to.

Consent as a Long-Term Relationship: Lessons for Longitudinal Studies

Stephanie Cargill is an associate professor of health care ethics at St. Louis University. She took a theoretical approach to question assumptions and frameworks in order to better achieve the goals of longitudinal research, especially with aging populations. She related that her work in the ethics of biobanking, biobanking consent, biobanking in communities, as well as challenges to traditional informed consent paradigms, apply to longitudinal studies in aging populations.

Cargill identified two central challenges unique to longitudinal studies: even if people understand the complex information about consent, the informational landscape very likely will change, meaning what the study will be doing and the risks might shift. In addition to the fact that the participants will probably change location over time, their values, priorities, and identities in a deeper sense might be different, which is problematic if the ethical onus rests on information and choice provided at the very beginning. Another challenge of consent in longitudinal studies is the issue of withdrawal and retention, she explained, which is a tension between the right and the ability for people to withdraw and the scientific validity of longitudinal studies that requires retention over periods of time.

As Cargill related, historically there have been many critiques of the traditional notion of consent, in which most of the ethical work of consent happens at a discrete event where someone is given information and then makes a choice. Consent is usually assumed to be unidirectional, meaning that the researchers or members of the research team provide information actively and have the responsibility for the information and context being appropriate, and the participants are seen as somewhat passive receivers. Even though the participants need to understand and choose, the responsibilities lay primarily on the givers of the information. Barriers to consent are often participants' understanding or environmental factors, such as whether there is sufficient time or participants feel safe in that environment.

Cargill noted that for longitudinal studies, this model of the ethics of consent is problematic because researchers cannot provide enough information at the outset since neither they nor the participants know for sure what will happen in the future. To her, framing people as passive receivers of an intervention does not work if they are to be active in their consent and participation over time. Other models, such as broad consent, do not solve these problems because they do not provide an informed choice nor are people more active participants.

Cargill briefly reviewed alternative models of consent, emphasizing that the ongoing process of informed consent is more than checking back in with people. Rather, it means that consent is ethically valid over time and part of an ongoing relationship between the researchers and their participants in terms of information and choice (Lidz et al., 1988). She cited Miller and Wertheimer (2010), who made an even deeper point that not only should consent be a process, but also it is a bidirectional process. Rather than the researchers holding all the responsibility for consent and making sure all the information is provided, there are responsibilities on both sides so participants make the choice that is appropriate to them.

Cargill's work draws on the health communication literature, she said, making the argument that consent is a communication process. She argued that a very antiquated notion of how communication works is used by many researchers seeking consent. Known as the transmission model of communication, where there is a sender and a receiver and noise, this model of communication was rejected by scholars and researchers long ago, she said. Modern communication theories are much more complex and involve the relationship, the trust, the deferral of authority, the shaping of identities, and other concerns. She challenged workshop participants to think about what it means to be in an ethical relationship with people in longitudinal studies, and what it means for information and choice. Cargill said that for people to continue to participate ethically in longitudinal studies, they need to continue to make the choice to be in it. Both sides need to forge a relationship. She called for knowing what makes people want to be in, and continue to want to be in, these studies.

Alternative consent models lessen the ethical pressure to make sure at the beginning that all the information is given, it is understood, and consent is completely voluntary, all in that one discrete moment in time, Cargill said. These models lessen the pressure because information will continue to be disclosed, and choices will continue to be made. However, she cautioned that these models also require that researchers pay attention to the communities and populations with whom they are working and invest in a relationship with them. Trust needs to be built at the outset with access to desired information over time, she emphasized. Ways are needed to motivate people to continue, whether incentives or other types of services, but withdrawal has to be accessible as well.

Cargill provided some implications for studies on aging populations and emphasized that researchers should do their "homework" and think carefully about aging populations in different contexts with different capacities. She urged researchers to consider what people would want to know to make their initial decisions, what would motivate them to continue or to stop, and what is the best way to communicate. The bidirectional aspect of consent means that information needs to be gathered and given on both sides, she emphasized; not only are researchers giving information to participants, but also participants need to give information to researchers so the study can be designed in a way that accommodates and forges the correct relationship.

Cargill concluded that from an Institutional Review Board perspective, this type of consent is not so radically different that it does not satisfy the regulations. Researchers need to understand the risk level to argue for the nature of the initial consent in the process and for revisiting consent with funding built in. She suggested researchers can justify this consent by citing evidence that it increases retention.

Ethical Considerations for Obtaining Informed Consent in Longitudinal Studies of Aging

Emily Largent is the Emanuel and Robert Hart Assistant Professor of Medical Ethics and Health Policy at the University of Pennsylvania, and she holds a secondary appointment at the Penn Law School. Her research focuses on Alzheimer's disease, and she said she has been keenly aware of the ethical challenges that arise when participants have or—as can occur in longitudinal studies of aging—may be expected to experience cognitive or functional impairment. Because it is important to include cognitively impaired older adults in studies, she said it is necessary to identify strategies to approach the consent process thoughtfully.

Largent noted that obtaining consent for research participation is a way of demonstrating respect for people, and it allows them to decide for themselves whether participating in research is consistent with their values, preferences, and interests. But, she said, individuals experiencing cognitive impairment typically experience an erosion of their ability to self-determine, i.e., to make choices about what they do and what happens to them. Largent pointed out this potential mismatch between the goals of informed consent for research and participants' abilities to grant consent.

Largent highlighted three ethical considerations arising from this mismatch. First, researchers need a clear plan for assessing decision-making capacity and, in the event they discover that an older adult they are seeking to enroll lacks capacity, for ensuring the individual's voice is still heard in the consent process. Second, researchers need to appreciate the challenges that arise from recruiting dyads that are comprised of a research participant and the research participant's study partner. Third, researchers need to think about the importance of using the consent process to set participants' expectations regarding the return of results.

In longitudinal studies of aging, some individuals will reasonably be expected to experience cognitive changes, she pointed out, and a goal of the research may be to examine how cognition changes over time. She noted that capacity is task and context specific and can fluctuate, waxing and waning over time, so a diagnosis of dementia does not necessarily mean that an individual lacks capacity. Tests of cognitive abilities may be predictive of decisional abilities, she explained, but typically are not appropriate for gauging capacity. She also warned researchers not to rely on staff, such as those in a long-term care facility, to tell them who or who does not have the capacity to consent to research participation.

Largent said that for all of these reasons, investigators need to go into a study with a robust plan for how to assess prospective participants' capacity to consent to research. She encourages them to engage in a dialog that includes opportunities for prospective participants to repeat back key concepts about the research, including what it involves and how participation might affect them. The investigator's assessment of those answers, whether adequate or inadequate, helps inform a final determination of capacity. If the participant does not have capacity, the investigator typically needs to identify an appropriate surrogate decision maker, which can be a challenge and can constitute an obstacle to recruiting a representative sample.

Largent also noted that even if a surrogate provides permission for an older adult to participate in research, the investigator's job, from an ethical perspective, is still not done because decision-making capacity requires understanding, appreciation, reasoning, and the ability to evidence a choice. Individuals who do not have capacity still may have one or more of these constituent abilities to a meaningful extent, she said. So, she continued, individuals with diminished capacity should generally be asked for their assent or they should be given an opportunity to dissent from participation in research, even if the researcher has already obtained permission from a surrogate decision maker. Because assent and dissent are big concepts, she urges investigators to plan not just for a capacity assessment, but how they will operationalize the idea of assent and dissent in practice or in the field.

Largent went on to note that in longitudinal studies, participants might experience cognitive decline and therefore diminished capacity as the study continues. In these instances, study visits should be seen as ongoing opportunities to check in with participants and ensure that continued participation is something that they are interested in and willing to do. In her view, formal reconsent to participation is not necessary unless there is a material change in information, such as changes in the risk-benefit balance, burdens, or if other material information becomes available. When additional consents are requested, such as a physical exam or biospecimen collection, Largent said a new capacity assessment may be necessary.

Largent suggested that researchers conducting longitudinal studies of aging may wish to consider alternative mechanisms, such as research advance directives, for participants to express their research-related wishes should they become incapacitated. Research advance directives are not widely used, she acknowledged, but they can be useful in sparking discussion among family members who may not otherwise have an opportunity to discuss an individual's preferences regarding research participation. In addition, completion of a research advance directive can be an opportunity to identify a surrogate to make decisions about research participation. To Largent, such a document might actually change the view or the kinds of research that can permissibly be conducted with individuals who lack decision-making capacity.

Turning to dyads, Largent explained aging research and Alzheimer's disease research often require that individuals enroll with a study partner who is a knowledgeable informant and can provide information about the participant's cognition and function. That information is sometimes used to determine study eligibility, but it can also be used to assess various outcome measures. Study partners can also play important roles in managing study logistics, providing transportation to an appointment, ensuring the participant has the appointment on their calendar, and monitoring the participant in between study visits. The partner is particularly important if there is an intervention, such as an investigational new drug, and the study is looking for side effects. A partner can also help ensure adherence to a study protocol. She noted that studies show that the decision to participate in research is often made collaboratively within a participant's study partner dyad. Unsurprisingly, cognitively unimpaired older adults tend to make these decisions more independently, but they still talk about engaging with trusted others to discuss research participation.

Largent noted that dyads in which the research participant has either mild cognitive impairment or a dementia-level impairment may still engage in a highly collaborative process between the participant and the study partner, although the study partner takes on a more dominant role in decision making as the participant's cognitive decline continues. This observation leads to an important consideration in recruitment and retention strategies that target the research participant as well as the study partner, she commented. She finds many study partners appreciate a call from the investigator to explain the study and its requirements so that they can see the value of the study and understand the value they are contributing to it. Flexible scheduling of appointments, telephone and video visits, and reimbursement and incentives for study partners should be considered, she added.

Largent cautioned that if having a study partner is an eligibility criterion, structural barriers, such as an adult child who is still in the workforce or taking care of their own family, make it harder to participate in research, leading to a lack of representativeness. Requiring a study partner would wholly exclude some populations, particularly unfriended older adults, an important population that has unmet needs and is worthy of research. She also said that triadic communication between a patient, family member, and a researcher can be a challenge for individuals with cognitive impairment because these individuals often feel like they are left out of a conversation—that people talk past them or about them, instead of with them. Investigators need strategies for ensuring that they are talking with and receiving information from both members of a dyad, she urged.

Largent next highlighted the return of results, which may include genetic testing results, biomarker results, and cognitive testing results, among others. These results can provide insight into risk of cognitive and functional decline, reveal the presence of pathology, or illuminate changes over time, hinting perhaps at prognosis. Based on her research, Largent said older adults often value having this information and use it in different ways, including for their own health and health care decision making. For example, individuals who learn about their increased risk for Alzheimer's disease report that they exercise more, eat fewer processed foods, and play brain games. Even when information is not viewed by older adults as being medically actionable, she continued, it may still have importance for life planning purposes. Participants may update wills and advance directives, make choices about working longer or retiring sooner, or engage in financial planning in anticipation of future care needs, she pointed out. Conversely, people who find that they are at less risk than they initially assumed for developing cognitive impairment due to Alzheimer's disease talk about being reassured and feeling that they have a freer future in which to plan.

Largent said that information about risk diagnosis and prognosis is not just of interest to the older adult, but also to family members who might learn something about their own health. This is particularly clear when an older adult learns genetic information and shares it with genetic relatives. Family members might also learn something about their risk of caregiving, she added, which can change their own health behaviors and future plans.

With this background, Largent said that the consent process needs to be understood as an opportunity to set participants' expectations about the return of results: Will results be shared at all? If so, which results, with whom, and under what conditions? An investigator's offer to share clinically validated results can serve as a powerful incentive to participate in research. In addition, many participants feel the information is theirs and they are entitled to it, although others may prefer not to know. She emphasized making sure the consent process helps people understand what the results are and if results will be coming to them, and that information needs to be provided in the informed consent document.

Largent concluded that longitudinal studies of aging constitute an important means of understanding and addressing the needs of older adults and their family members; however, obtaining consent in such studies, particularly when individuals are at risk for or experiencing impaired decisional capacity, can be ethically challenging.

Ethical Considerations for Obtaining Informed Consent: Insights from Psychology

Sunita Sah is a professor and organizational psychologist at Cornell University. She shared insights from psychology, behavioral economics, and her own research to draw implications for longitudinal survey consent. She echoed the five elements for valid consent that Grady and other ethical and legal commentators have identified: consent should be voluntary, not coerced; people must have cognitive ability, the capacity to consent and not be impaired in any way; people should receive sufficient information on the risks, benefits, and the alternatives; and they should have an adequate understanding of the disclosed facts. Finally, they must either authorize, give informed consent, or decline by giving an informed refusal.

While it is necessary that the consent process provide disclosures of relevant information, Sah said her focus is on whether some disclosures have an impact on the other elements that are needed for valid consent, in particular the voluntary element. Her research has examined disclosures of potential risk, which can produce unintended burdens due to unexpected psychological effects that can occur.

To Sah, disclosure's great promise is that it provides potentially useful information so that recipients can make an informed choice. However, she has uncovered some unintended consequences from disclosure. She asked the workshop audience to imagine going to a doctor who recommends that they enter into a clinical trial, but the doctor says that under disclosure rules, the doctor is required to disclose stock ownership in the company of this drug. Sah asked the audience: How does that make you feel? What do you do with that information? How do you respond to the doctor? She noted the likelihood of feeling extremely uncomfortable about signaling distrust in this type of situation or insinuating that the doctor could be biased or corrupt in any way.

Without disclosure of the conflict of interest, Sah posited, patients could present a range of reasons for rejecting the trial, including it sounds too risky, it is too painful, or that it may have undesirable side effects. After the doctor has disclosed a conflict of interest, it becomes salient that the refusal is more likely to be interpreted as being due to the disclosure, and this signals distrust in the doctor.

Sah described two psychological processes that increase pressure to comply with others, even when there is a decrease in trust. Insinuation anxiety is the reluctance to signal distrust due to the fear of insinuating that the other person is untrustworthy. She described it as an aversive, emotional state that occurs when people become concerned about offending the other person and implying they are something different than what they appear to be. She said that insinuation anxiety can have a great impact on behavior.

Another psychological process, called the panhandler effect, arises from pressure to help someone out and not wanting to appear unhelpful.

Sah said that both insinuation anxiety and the panhandler effect could appear in the same situation or sometimes only one is present. Both are tied to relationship concerns and pressures to not signal distrust or unhelpfulness, and both processes contribute to what she refers to as the burden-of-disclosure effect. The two forces work in opposing directions as to whether the person will take the advice or not. A person is placed in an effective bind about whether or not to follow advice or a recommendation. Sah said that the person is stuck between a rock and a hard place. Instead of being the warning that it is supposed to be, disclosure of potential risk can put a burden on those that it is supposed to protect, increasing the pressure to comply with recommendations.

Sah described a study where she tested these two hypotheses. Study participants, asked to take the perspective of patients, read about a common situation that they might encounter at a doctor's office and they listened to their doctor give two options. The doctor gives the same recommendations in all the conditions. She introduced one situation as follows:

> Imagine you are a patient suffering from early onset arthritis, and you've been seeing your rheumatologist, Dr. McLane, who you have known for the last three years. You are currently suffering from an acute attack which has left some of your joints aching and swollen. You decide to pay a visit to your doctor. After examining you and reviewing some of your test results, Dr. McLane says...

Sah said that participants then listen to a voice recording where the doctor recommends either entering a clinical trial or using a standard drug. There are two options, and the doctor always recommends entering the trial. In the disclosure condition, one more sentence is added to the voice recording, which is when the doctor discloses the financial conflict of interest. In this option, the doctor says, "I do think it is important, however, to let you know I will receive a referral fee from the manufacturer of the drug if I refer you for the clinical trial."

Sah said that in the disclosure condition she saw a significantly decreased amount of trust in the doctor, but at the same time, reports of increased insinuation anxiety. She noted that both trust and insinuation anxiety matter when making a decision about whether or not to follow the advice. She also drew a distinction between compliance and consent; compliance is not valid consent, and it is unreliable and short lived. She referred to other studies that showed once people have an opportunity to change their mind in private, compliance drops immediately, and they reverse their decision. She said that this suggests an element of feeling coerced, which decreases the aspect of voluntariness, a critical element of valid consent.

In another study, Sah and colleagues sought to increase consent but reduce insinuation anxiety. They added two additional conditions, one in which the doctor states that the disclosure is legally required and one in which a written disclosure is given to the patient by someone else before seeing the doctor. Her results showed that any disclosure decreased trust, regardless of whether it was voluntary, required by law, or given by someone else. However, insinuation anxiety is much higher if the disclosure is given face-to-face by the doctor, regardless whether it is seen as voluntary or required by law, and insinuation anxiety decreases when the disclosure is given by someone else.

Sah next described a large randomized preregistered field study conducted at Cleveland Clinic, taking advantage of a policy change about to be introduced that required physicians who received $20,000 or more from industry to disclose this information to patients. The researchers manipulated the policy change in a large field study of over 1,900 patients at two different outpatient clinics through a letter that either just scheduled an appointment (control condition) or included a disclosure of a financial conflict, with a detailed explanation on the second page about which companies the doctor had conflicts. The letter also manipulated whether patients received information on the risks, the benefits, or both of their physician having a financial relationship with the company.

Sah said that they were interested in whether, after receiving this letter, patients would go to their appointment, cancel it, or just not show up. Those patients who did see their physician were sent a survey within a week of their appointment. They obtained a 68 percent response rate for the survey, which tested patients' knowledge and understanding of the information in the disclosure letter, as well as trust in the physician and the hospital. Seventy-two percent of the patients remembered receiving the letter, and 57 percent of people in the disclosure condition said they knew their physician had a conflict of interest. They found no effects on trust in the physician and the hospital in any of the conditions, or on appointment attendance.

Sah concluded by noting the implications of research to improve consent and retention and to reduce insinuation anxiety. To decrease the pressure, external disclosure works well. Giving the disclosure ahead of time, making sure it is salient, and making sure people understand that they can deliberate would help reduce insinuation anxiety, she said.

Discussion

Thompson asked John Phillips to launch the discussion. He asked Sah about the context of her study on disclosure of financial conflicts of interest. He asked about any comparable issue in recruiting participants for a longitudinal aging study where there does not seem to be any financial conflict that would arise. He inquired whether incentive payments might be equivalent to a financial conflict.

Sah suggested thinking about the issue in terms of how uncertainty and how risks are presented. In additional studies where it was clear that the person asking does not have any personal agenda, she posited that the direct application is the balance of risks and benefits that are being communicated and how they are communicated. For example, if risks are communicated face-to-face, people have other unintended burdens placed on them. They might want to ask more questions or feel very uncomfortable with the risks, but dismiss them because of relationship concerns. Having time to deliberate beforehand and providing information about risks and benefits in a balanced way would increase valid consent and retain participants, she suggested, rather than obtaining consent on the spot and then having participants change their mind later.

Grady pointed out people have different incentives for participating, and they react very differently. Some participants believe if a large financial incentive is offered, then there is more risk involved in taking part in the study. Others are very persuaded by financial incentives. Sah posited how risks are communicated, whether face-to-face or whether people have time to focus on them, would be the biggest takeaway.

Phillips asked whether giving people time to leave and think about participating means that they might not come back. Sah replied that it will increase valid consent. She noted Jäckle also had evidence that when people have more time to deliberate, the more reflective people will end up consenting as opposed to giving a kneejerk reaction on the spot to consent because they feel pressured and then decline later.

Thompson asked the panel of presenters what they saw as the most pressing research needs. Grady said for each population or each kind of study, a better understanding is needed about what would motivate people and why they would care about participating. She referred to Cargill's community engagement work and suggested it provides an important homework assignment for any study.

Cargill said that they have done a number of studies on the quality of the decision at the time of consent, but people make those decisions at very different times. She said some studies show that people have already decided when they walk in the door about whether they will do the study. She noted that once people have decided they will do something, they are not open to different information, and getting them to listen to the pros and cons is very difficult. She urged more understanding about how people make decisions through time as opposed to just in the immediate moment.

Phillips told Largent the idea of a study partner is compelling, but some people will not be able to get a study partner for various reasons. He asked about research or experience with the ways in which that challenge has been overcome. Largent replied that she and colleagues do a lot of work with study partners and try to understand who can and cannot find a study partner. They have found almost everyone can identify one person who might be willing to be a study partner, but typically it is only one person. As soon as people encounter an obstacle to asking that person to be their partner, quite a few participants are lost; it is much easier for people who are married and have a retired spouse. It varies by study, she commented, but researchers need to consider whether a study partner is necessary and whether there are other ways to gather information.

Phillips asked Cargill about getting ongoing consent and whether repeatedly asking participants if they want to be in the study makes them more likely to drop out. He questioned the risk of this approach for longitudinal studies. Cargill identified two kinds of longitudinal studies: in some cases, people provide samples and data, and the researcher wants to be allowed to continue to use it. This case provides an incentive to stay under the radar, because as long as they are not reminded, they are not going to withdraw. If they are reminded, there is a higher chance that they will drop out. However, Cargill called for a paradigm shift for longitudinal studies that requires continuous participation to think about how to motivate people to continue. She said that this is where community engagement comes in: People continue because they are getting something out of it. The key question, she said, is lessening the burden for people to continue or making them want to continue because they get something out of it. She said those ways improve retention without a researcher simply hoping that participants will forget, because that is not ethical consent.

Phillips asked if there is any concern about panel effects, such as providing research findings on the impact of managing diet on health that may result in participants changing their diets as a result. He noted how much people change their behavior based on this kind of information is not known, but the question comes up often and raises concerns about whether a true random sample is maintained. Cargill said that it is worth thinking carefully about what type of information is provided to participants to not undermine the data. She pointed to many different ways to provide added value to participants besides narrowly telling them the results of the study. It could be information about other areas of their lives, for example, but said it is important to do the homework and ask people what would motivate them to continue and what they would like to gain from the study.

5

Data Linkage and Innovation

This chapter summarizes the presentations and discussions in the workshop sessions on data linkage and innovation. Jennifer Madans chaired the session on data linkage, and Michael Davern chaired the innovation session. Discussion followed each session.

DATA LINKAGE

Challenges to Connecting Data Across Agencies

Beth Virnig is a professor at the University of Minnesota and director of the Research Data Assistance Center (ResDAC) at the University of Minnesota, which is funded by a contract from the Centers for Medicare & Medicaid Services (CMS) to provide assistance to academic, government, and nonprofit researchers interested in using Medicare and Medicaid data for their research. Virnig clarified that she is not speaking for CMS but drawing on her experience using CMS data. She also explained that CMS manages the Medicare program, but works with states to manage the Medicaid programs. Medicaid is a partnership between CMS and the states, and each state is a little different. While CMS distributes Medicaid data, it does not directly collect the data.

One of the advantages of CMS data is its strong enrollment information, Virnig noted; information on everyone enrolled in each program is provided on a monthly basis, which provides a denominator for this population as well as some demographic information, and dates of birth and death. CMS has health claims data that include records—depending on the file, they are called bills, claims, or encounters—for health services limited to covered benefits. Some patients also have assessment data if they are in skilled nursing facilities, receive home health care visits, or receive inpatient rehab services.

Virnig reminded workshop participants about CMS's strict policies around linkage: There are a limited number of possible matching variables, and CMS will not release names or exact addresses. CMS conducts the linkage by sending a "finder file" to a contractor, and the CMS contractor returns validated matches. She noted that the contractor will return a validated match if a single match in the CMS file is identified, but if two or more potential matches are equally likely identified, then no data will be provided. Thus, the quality of the matching variables is very important, she stressed.

Virnig said that for linking to Medicare data, the best linking variable is a Social Security number (SSN), which is defined as either the personal SSN or the SSN to justify benefits. A Medicare Beneficiary ID was assigned to all beneficiaries after 2018, because of concerns about fraud and the elderly losing Medicare cards that revealed their SSNs. For matches prior to 2018, there is a Health Insurance Claim number, which is the SSN plus a couple of digits. She reminded researchers that if they are collecting this information over time, the meaning of the information has changed. A link can also be made on a name plus date of birth, but a name can be problematic as a linking variable.

Matching to state Medicaid data is different than Medicare. Virnig explained every state uses its own Medicaid ID that can be problematic to link to. There is no national standard and in some cases, people have IDs in more than one state or multiple Medicaid IDs in the same state. Virnig noted that while an SSN is often a preferred linking variable, not all states collect SSNs and not all states send SSNs to CMS. She said it is also possible, but problematic, to match using name plus date of birth.

Virnig shared examples of alignment of Medicare data with data from several studies to illustrate how Medicare complemented or supported the data collected in a survey. Figure 5-1 shows the Iowa Women's Health Study, which started in 1987. The red line shows mortality; the black line shows survey respondents; the blue line shows Medicare enrollments, some of whom aged into the program; and the light gray shows people who were both a current respondent and a current Medicare enrollee. According to Virnig, this figure illustrates a more dynamic way of thinking about linkages and the fact that surveys and linkages each work on their own rhythm and it is important to think about how the rhythms fit together.

Virnig noted that one of the challenges of linkages with Medicare data is a left truncation, which is the gap before a person is on Medicare. It is unknown what happened before the person was 65 years old; after age 65,

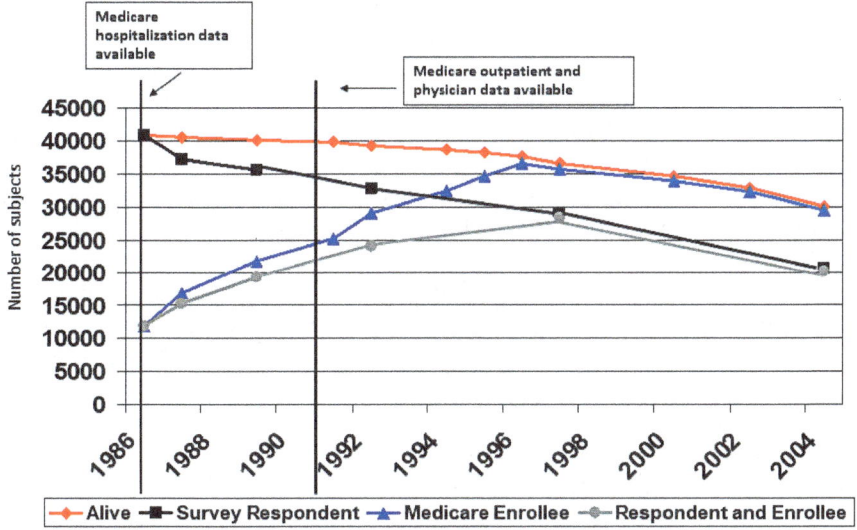

FIGURE 5-1 Availability of survey and Medicare data.
SOURCE: Beth Virnig workshop presentation, September 27, 2021.

their Medicare data are available. She said it is important to keep this in mind when trying to use Medicare data to assess attrition or look at nonresponse, as it may affect different parts of the population over time.

Another challenge with Medicaid data, Virnig said, is interval censoring, which is a mix of observations and gaps when people become enrolled on Medicaid, then may lose their eligibility and disappear. Later, they get their eligibility back, and their data can again be seen. She posited that people who cycle in and out of Medicaid may be of interest, and perhaps many of them are survey nonrespondents.

In addition to left truncation and interval censoring limiting the usefulness of linking to Medicare and Medicaid data, Virnig added that another area that likely needs more investigation is the impact of linking on survey sampling weights.

Virnig highlighted important issues for researchers when using Medicare claims data. These issues include some key variables, including demographic variables; coverage options, which identifies whether the person is enrolled in a managed care plan or has "fee for service"; diagnosis codes, using ICD (International Classification of Diseases)-9 or ICD-10; the dates of service; procedures performed, using ICD-9/ICD-10 or Current Procedural Terminology (CPT)/Healthcare Common Procedural Coding System (HCPCS) codes; types of care received, such as emergency room services, hospice, or rehabilitation services; and providers and locations of care. The data are collected in real time, and are not subject to recall bias like survey data can be, she pointed out, but there is no correction of past errors such as misdiagnosis. For example, there is no way to go back to January 2020, when COVID-19 diagnosis codes did not exist, to identify deaths that may have been due to COVID-19.

In addition, Virnig pointed out the data record what was done, and not what should have been done or what was intended to be done; as she said, one knows what happened but one does not know what did not happen. She also cautioned about using claims-based measures. For example, the codes for smoking are required to access smoking cessation services but not required otherwise, so they may not be a reliable indicator of smoking behavior. Conditions that are underdiagnosed in clinical settings, such as dementia, will be underrepresented in claims, she added.

Virnig described the need to create variables from the claims data, and noted some advantages and disadvantages. The flexibility provides tremendous opportunity but can be overwhelming. The dates of a survey can be used to sequence the survey with the claims. The claims data can show what was happening around the time that a survey was sent, and may reveal reasons for survey nonresponse. For example, a study that showed a hip fracture occurred around the time of the survey was very strongly associated with nonresponse.

Virnig briefly outlined the structure of different Medicare files, including the percentage of beneficiaries who have records in a given year and the median number of records per beneficiary. The Master Beneficiary Summary File has one record per enrollee per year, but other files are structured to provide one record per hospitalization or per bill, plus additional segments. The structure provides tremendous richness but can be overwhelming to manage, she commented.

To conclude, Virnig noted that payment and reporting policies change, codes change and are updated, and policies vary by state and time. She also pointed to the CMS reuse policy, and said it was particularly important to review for collaborative projects. ResDAC, the center at the University of Minnesota that she directs, can help researchers interested in CMS data.

The NCHS Data Linkage Program: Connecting Data Across Agencies

Lisa Mirel is the chief of the Data Linkage Methodology and Analysis Branch at the National Center for Health Statistics (NCHS), the nation's principal health statistics agency. In describing the data linkage program at NCHS, Mirel provided four examples of pressing policy questions that require complex and detailed data that NCHS has addressed by combining survey and administrative data:

1. Do Social Security Disability Insurance beneficiaries have access to care during the waiting period before Medicare entitlement?
2. Are there adverse health effects associated with the mandatory folic acid fortification policy for grain products?
3. How effective are health and housing policies in reducing lead exposure?
4. How likely are women and children who receive federal assisted housing to participate in the Special Supplemental Nutrition Program for Women, Infants, and Children?

Mirel said that data linkage is a very powerful mechanism that can provide policy-relevant information in an efficient way. She explained NCHS collects survey data to gather information about people's health status, health behaviors, and health care access. Administrative data are collected for programmatic purposes. NCHS then links data from the surveys with different sources of administrative data to create opportunities to answer key health and policy-relevant questions.

Surveys in NCHS linkage program include the National Health Interview Survey (NHIS), which is a nationally representative cross-sectional household survey that serves as an important source of information on the health of the civilian noninstitutionalized population in the United States; the National Health and Nutrition Examination Survey (NHANES), which is also a nationally representative, cross-sectional sample of the U.S. noninstitutionalized population that combines household-collected interview data with data collected at a mobile examination center; and the National Health Care Survey, which is a family of data collection efforts that gather information about providers, health care services, and patients across the health care spectrum.

Mirel described the key data elements that are collected as part of NCHS surveys, focusing on the household surveys, NHIS, and NHANES. Information is collected on health behaviors, including dietary intake, exercise, consumption of alcohol, and smoking; information on health conditions, based on what a doctor told the respondent in NHIS or actual physical measures in NHANES; socioeconomic information, including education and income; and information about health care access and utilization.

Mirel described some of the key sources of linked administrative data. The addresses of survey participants are geocoded to add in contextual information obtained from standard Census geocoded areas. Person-level data have been linked to data from the Department of Housing and Urban Development to identify survey respondents who are receiving federal-assisted housing, as well as the timing and type of housing assistance. Linkages with CMS data provided information on health care utilization and expenditures for survey participants who are receiving benefits from

CMS. The most utilized linkage is mortality, in which data from survey respondents are linked with the National Death Index (NDI) maintained by NCHS. This linkage can provide longitudinal follow-up for someone who was surveyed earlier to find out whether or not the person has died by the end of the follow-up interval. The NDI also contains information about the cause of death.

Mirel also described upcoming linkages, such as linking to data from the Department of Veterans Affairs (VA), with the hope those data are available for researchers in early 2022. She noted that researchers could use these linked data to answer questions about the health characteristics, health outcomes, and health care utilization for veterans who are using services within and outside the VA health system.

Mirel said that they will also link to the Transformed Medicaid Statistical Information System (T-MSIS) data from CMS, with an expected released in early 2022. She noted that they have previously linked Medicaid data through 2014, and T-MSIS will provide more recent data. Researchers can look at effects of changes in health care policy on the health status of Medicaid recipients.

In the next month, Mirel continued, a file will be released that includes survey participants who linked to end stage renal disease (ESRD) data from the National Institute on Diabetes and Digestive and Kidney Diseases. Although a very small subset of the population, as less than 1 percent have ESRD, it is a very important group because they account for about 7 percent of all Medicare spending. Researchers could use these data along with NHANES to examine the association of dietary intake with diagnosed ESRD.

Mirel said that the linkage program has been spending a lot of time to try to create sources that will support evidence building and make those data available to researchers. Also taking time are documentation and providing support to researchers about the linkage methodology to provide transparency into how these files are created. An assessment of the quality of the linkages is shared so researchers can assess potential linkage errors. NCHS also provides analytic guidelines for researchers on key variables and sample weights. Documentation is included on how these weights could be adjusted given the linkage, and how to interpret the findings based on the sample weights being representative at the time when the survey was conducted.

NCHS releases curated data files that can be used for many different research questions and more than 1,000 publications have been based on NCHS linked data, Mirel said. Each linked data file has a bibliography on the NCHS website. She highlighted the availability of NCHS linked data from NHIS and NHANES and the amount of follow-up longitudinal information: for the NDI, close to 35 years for participants who were in

NHIS in 1986; for NHANES, about 30 years. Mirel showed that for the linkages with Medicare and Medicaid data, there are about 25 years for some survey participants from NHIS and 20 years for NHANES. Similarly for linkages with the HUD data, they have almost 20 years of follow-up for both surveys.

Mirel next focused on challenges and opportunities in linking data. Agreements for data sharing are often one of the biggest challenges. Issues that arise in discussions about linkages with other agencies include who will own the final linked dataset, where the dataset will reside, how the linkage will occur, and where the linkage will occur.

Another challenge is linkage methodology, Mirel said. NCHS collects personally identifiable information (PII) as part of its survey and the administrative record has that information as well, so they usually link based on PII. Some privacy concerns arise about sharing direct identifiers, and her group has looked into privacy-preserving record linkage (PPRL) approaches that would mask the PII and create hash tokens so an exchange of PII to do the linkage would never occur. She said that they have validated the results of the PPRL methods against their standard methodologies and are hoping to use this validation to expand the data sources for linking.

In terms of the quality of linked data, Mirel stressed the quality of the PII reported in the surveys is very important, so they look at some standards and assessment tools when doing the linkage. Machine learning techniques are improving linkage efficiency and external sources can help validate the linkages. In addition, NCHS has examined selection bias for cases that are eligible for linkage in the NHIS and suggested ways to mitigate that bias through adjusting sample weights.

The final challenge that Mirel touched on was accessibility of the linked data files. Because linked data put participants at a greater risk of re-identification, NCHS has been working on creating more publicly available linked data sources using synthetic data and then setting up a validation server so that researchers could validate their results from the synthetic data against the true data. She said that they are hoping to conduct meetings with researchers to identify key variables and create analytically useful datasets. Interactive data visualization tools and other ways to increase accessibility of these linked data for evidence building are also under consideration.

In Mirel's opinion, successful data linkage rests on three main factors: support and adequate resources from both entities that are going to be involved in the linkage process, consensus on data management responsibilities, and agreement on where researchers can obtain secure access once the files are put together. She concluded by noting some additional uses of linked data, including using information from administrative sources to improve survey operations, such as by improving questionnaire design or identifying people who had died in advance of data collection for potential follow-up studies.

Discussion

Jennifer Madans, noting that both presenters mentioned challenges as well as opportunities that address the future of data linkage, asked Virnig and Mirel what they think is most important to address now to take full advantage of linkage, both to enhance the availability of data for substantive analysis and to address selection bias.

Mirel replied that agreements for data sharing are one of the biggest obstacles; she suggested using PPRL could open the door to linking to potentially many more sources without needing the direct exchange of PII.

Virnig suggested developing ways to help build teams to work on complex projects involving surveys and administrative data linkages. People typically know only one of the data sources, yet expertise is required for both the survey and the administrative data, which each have their own complexities. John Phillips commented that many longitudinal studies sponsored by the National Institute on Aging (NIA) have long provided linkages to Social Security Administration (SSA) records and to CMS records. Although documentation exists, he acknowledged those data files are not easy for researchers to use and agreed that team building and networks could help facilitate research.

Phillips asked Mirel about the consent process for NHANES with the biological data and administrative linkages: that is, whether it is a general consent or multiple consents for the different linkages and biodata collection. A number of questions for consent are placed at the beginning of the household survey, Mirel replied, including a specific question to ask for consent for linkage when participants are invited to take part in the survey. Madans confirmed that there are multiple consents, very similar to other surveys described, and that consent to one piece does not automatically mean consent to all.

Phillips inquired about the success of the NHANES or NHIS consent process for administrative data. Requirements from SSA for consent has been a challenge for many NIA-supported studies, he said. Mirel responded that her group has spent a lot of time researching those issues, and that for NHIS prior to 2007, consent for linkage was implicit if respondents provided their SSNs, which they were told could be linked to other records. The procedure was changed in 2007, because in the years leading up to 2007, many more respondents refused to provide their SSNs. Based on research, the questionnaire in the NHIS was changed and participants were told about the linkage, the possible sources, and health-related research that could be done, then asked to provide the last four digits of their SSNs.

If respondents refused to provide the last four digits, they were asked for consent to link without an SSN. Prior to 2007, the consent rate for linkage was around 50 percent, whereas now it is in the high 80s, with about half providing the last four digits of their SSN and half consenting to linkage without providing an SSN. She noted that having all nine digits of the SSN makes linkages easier, but having limited PII can still work, although it required changes in the linkage methodology. In response to a follow-up from Phillips, Mirel said the last four digits of an SSN provide reasonably accurate linkages with other identifiers. She pointed to a research paper that looked at linkage eligibility bias for the people in the survey for whom they had all records, assessed what the bias was, and posited how to mitigate it with some adjustment to the sample weights.

Madans shared the difficult experience in negotiating for each administrative data source, noting each agency poses different and sometimes contradictory requirements. She wondered whether implementation of the Evidence Act would create the potential for stronger coordination and could provide a forum to bring together agencies with administrative data to work out agreements with statistical agencies. She also asked about any unintended consequences, and who could lead a coordination effort.

Phillips built on that question. He noted that some of the legal discussions around this issue equated an understanding of the consent process and the risks involved with the provision of a full SSN. He questioned this premise, pointing out SSA warns people not to give out their SSN. The Department of Health and Human Services Data Council might be an arena to have a discussion for standardization of study consent forms, he said.

Related discussions are taking place as part of the implementation of the Evidence Act and the National Secure Data Service, Mirel said, but the focus is on bringing different data sources together to answer specific questions. They have implications for studies that create curated files to address a wide variety of questions, but further discussions will be needed, she observed. Virnig added the Health Insurance Portability and Accountability Act (HIPAA) is another law important for CMS data and that some HIPAA requirements have been an impediment to linking data.

LOOKING AHEAD: APPLYING INNOVATIVE STRATEGIES TO IMPROVE CONSENT AND RESPONSE

Some Reflections on Improving Response and Consent

Annette Jäckle said although the theme of this workshop has been about how to improve consent and response in longitudinal studies of aging, she suggested reframing it around how to reconcile increasing demands for more data with what respondents are willing and able to provide. Understanding and meeting respondents' needs and preferences are necessary, she stressed.

Jäckle urged an understanding of what respondents think they have signed up for when they participate in a survey. She hypothesized that when participants agree to take part in an initial interview that is part of a panel study, they have an idea of what they think they have agreed to do. That perception influences what they think is an acceptable request or not and whether or not they will do additional things for the study. She also hypothesized that these perceptions are at least in part influenced by the design of the original survey.

If these hypotheses are true, Jäckle continued, then it is important to think about how to design the study for these additional tasks, including the survey, the consent question, and the incentives. The goal would be to design surveys to increase acceptability of additional requests that conform with what respondents think they signed up for so they agree to do the additional tasks.

Jäckle described results from methodological studies over the past years that point to these hypotheses, although research studies to explicitly test them have not yet been designed.

The first study was from the Innovation Panel of Understanding Society, a sample of 1,500 households in Great Britain in which all household members aged 16 and over are interviewed once a year (see Chapter 4). Part of the sample is allocated to computer assisted personal interview first and to web first; in both modes, there is a follow-up of nonrespondents in the other mode. Respondents were asked to download an app to record their spending every day for one month. They included an experiment on how respondents were invited to the app, with half the sample invited during the annual interview and half sent a letter several weeks after their interview.

Jäckle said that they saw no differences for the web respondents in the proportion who participate in this mobile app study regardless of how they were invited. Her interpretation is that people who do the survey by web see themselves as participating in a self-completion study, and the app is just one more item for completion; it is consistent with what they think they have signed up to do. Although participation was low (16 percent), how they were asked made no difference. The results were very different in face-to-face interviews. Only 9 percent responded to the mailed invitation, but 29 percent of respondents who received the invitation during the interview downloaded the app and provided spending data. She observed if the request was in the interview, it was seen as part of what they have agreed to do, whereas the mailed request was seen as something extra and different from what they think they agreed to do.

In a second study, also using the Innovation Panel, respondents were asked to download an app and use it every day for 14 days to answer questions about their experiences that day and their well-being. In this study, everyone was invited during their annual interview, but the researchers experimentally varied where in the interview the invitation occurred: half the sample got the invitation to the app relatively early in the questionnaire and the other half at the end. She reported a big difference: 33 percent of the respondents asked at the end of the interview agreed to download the app and logged in, but 44 percent of those asked earlier in the interview did so.

A COVID-19 study was conducted on the main sample of Understanding Society, Jäckle continued. Starting in April 2020, the study sent additional questionnaires about respondents' experiences during the pandemic (initially monthly, then every 2 months). In March 2021 they asked people for consent to link their survey data to health records, and they experimentally varied where in the survey respondents were asked for consent. Similar results were seen as the previous study: asking early in the survey yielded higher consent rates (76 percent) than asking at the end (68 percent). Among the people who were asked late and did not consent, 54 percent said it is because it was "Too personal, I've shared enough information with this survey." For those who were asked early, a smaller proportion (50 percent) gave that reason. Jäckle noted the consistent pattern of findings across different types of tasks suggest that if asked early in a survey, people are more willing to do additional things than if asked late. Although this may be fatigue, it may be that they feel they have already done enough.

Jäckle's last example was an experiment on incentives from the COVID-19 study. This study asked respondents for permission to send them a serology testing kit to check for COVID-19 antibodies, which they completed and returned. She focused on results comparing participants who received either £2 to complete the survey plus £5 if they returned the serology sample to those who received £7 pounds for the survey, with no bonus for returning the serology sample. Jäckle said that in the group that received £2 for the survey plus £5 for returning serology, 52 percent of respondents returned the test kit compared to 48 percent of those who were just promised £7 if they completed the survey. However, she noted that when they looked at the issued sample, they did not see any difference between the two because the response rate was higher in the £7 group. Higher participation occurred in the survey when they offered £7 than when they offered £2 plus £5.

To Jäckle, the question is what to place value on and how to communicate that value to respondents, whether the survey that includes the additional tasks or the individual tasks. She shared she has been reflecting on how the response to additional requests might be influenced by the design of the study in which the additional requests are made (Figure 5-2). Starting in the top left-hand corner of the figure, she directed workshop participants'

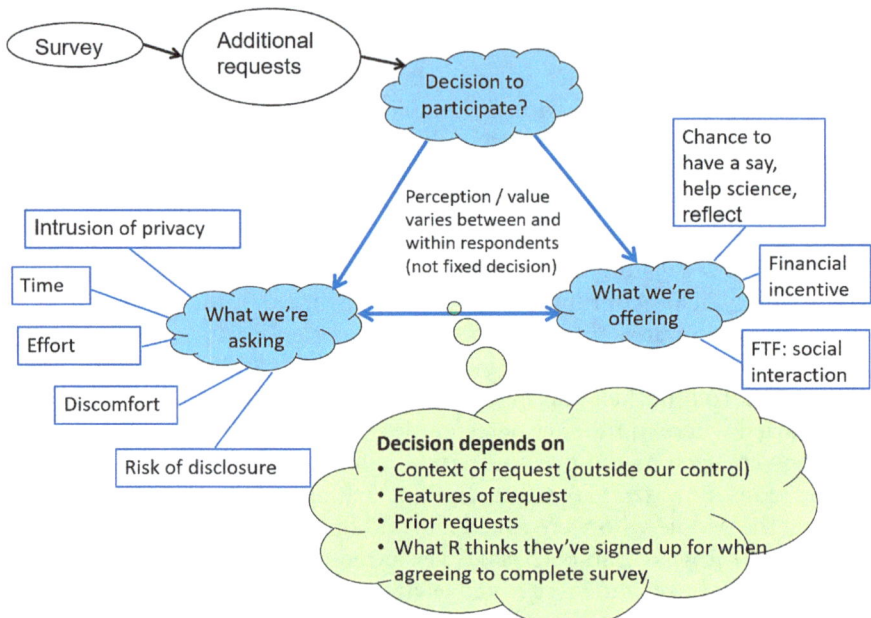

FIGURE 5-2 Model respondent's decision whether to participate in additional tasks.
SOURCE: Annette Jäckle workshop presentation, September 28, 2021.

attention to the survey questionnaire, then the additional requests made, such as for biosamples, additional measurements, and additional questionnaires. The respondent then has to decide whether or not to participate for each additional request.

Jäckle noted respondents are being asked for their time, their effort, and acceptance of some intrusion of privacy. Sometimes they must agree to accept some discomfort or do something that might trigger a fear (for example, if it involves needles), as well as accept a risk of disclosure, even if small. They are being offered a chance to have a say, help science, and receive a financial incentive. A face-to-face survey also offers a social interaction. She noted that each respondent will place a different value on each aspect, and people are willing to tolerate different amounts of burden and discomfort.

Jäckle noted that the decision whether or not to participate in these additional tasks depends on contextual factors outside of researchers' control and influence. However, the features of the request itself, such as wording of the request and the incentives provided, have an impact on consent for additional tasks. In addition, the tasks that respondents have already done and their perceptions of whether the additional request is consistent with what they think they have signed up to do also influence their decision.

Jäckle concluded that the goal is to design surveys in such a way that people find additional requests acceptable. The next steps are to think the process through theoretically; talk to respondents, including both people who consent and do not consent to additional requests; feed the comments into a theoretical framework; develop hypotheses; and test them experimentally.

From Consent to Linkage: New Data Infrastructure Payoffs

Timothy Smeeding is the Lee Rainwater Distinguished Professor of Public Affairs and Economics at the School of Public Affairs at the University of Wisconsin-Madison. In recent years, Smeeding has worked with CNSTAT and the National Academies committee members to develop the American Opportunity Study (AOS), which was the focus of his talk.[1]

Smeeding began by highlighting the payoffs from new data infrastructure and the issues of consent and linking to these resources. Smeeding said the AOS is quickly becoming a reality. He said that one of the biggest keys to linkage is Title 13 of the United States Code, which is the statute authorizing the Census Bureau and all of its work. The law prohibits disclosing or publishing private information that identifies individuals, or businesses, including names, addresses, SSNs, and telephone numbers. After 72 years, the data are released from Title 13 protection, and data from the 1850 to 1940 Censuses can and have been linked. He described how people use these 10-year panels for genealogy purposes. He shared a link to the Census Linking Project, which offers researchers information to create longitudinal datasets using historical Census data back from 90 years.[2] He noted that the 1950 Census reaches 72 years in 2022, at which time those data will be released publicly. More recent data and linkages are currently available only inside the Federal Statistical Research Data Centers (FSRDCs). Specifically, he said, data from the 2000 and 2010 Censuses are linked, and the linking for the data from the 1960 to 1990 Censuses is in progress.

A group of researchers have explored the historical linked data to examine the effects of the Civil War on intergenerational mortality and other topics, Smeeding said. He cited an article by Abramitzky et al. (2021) in the *Journal of Economic Literature* on automated linking of historical data, which looked at several different ways to do this linkage that provide 90 to 95 percent certainty of match. He called this an extraordinary opportunity

---

[1] For more information on the AOS development, see Grusky, Smeeding, and Snipp (2015), and Grusky, Hout, Smeeding, and Snipp (2019).
[2] See https://censuslinkingproject.org/ .

to create large, longitudinal datasets by linking individuals from one Census to another or from other sources like a survey through the Census Linking Project. A number of research papers are using these data, such as a paper on intergenerational mobility by race using data going back to 1850 (Ward, 2021).

Smeeding provided additional background and context about linking more recent Census data. The AOS was initiated in 2009 by Smeeding, David Grusky, Matt Snipp, and Mike Hout, with inspiration and funding connections from Bob Hauser, Sean Reardon, David Johnson, and Rob Mare. The goal of AOS is to take a current sample of people and look at their mobility over time, with data on their occupation, industry, income, and living arrangements. He noted that the way researchers have examined intergenerational mobility to date is to find people who were born in the 1950s, 1960s, and 1970s, and then wait until they are 45 or 50 and compare them with their parents. The Panel Study of Income Dynamics (PSID) and National Longitudinal Surveys (NLS) are examples. The AOS provides an alternative by starting in the present and looking back in time. The key is linking the 1960 through the 1990 Censuses, which are handwritten, and translating and digitizing them, Smeeding explained.

This would also open the chance to trace immigrant mobility of current cohorts by determining when their parents first emerged in the decennial Census, he continued. Every longitudinal survey begins with a given population, hence people first surveyed in the 1960s (PSID) or 1970s (NLS) form the core, and anyone who migrates to the United States after this start can only enter the survey by marriage or cohabitation with an original survey respondent.

The AOS standing committee at the National Academies conducted a study with Johnathan Fisher and others that found that records could be digitized with 93 percent accuracy. Raj Chetty helped raise money for this work, and the Decennial Census Digitization and Linkage (DCDL) project is under way.[3]

In summary, Smeeding explained that at an early meeting of a standing NAS committee on the AOS, David Johnson, who was chief of the Social, Economic and Housing Statistics Division in 2008, created a slide to show the possibilities of a Survey of Income and Program Participation gold standard file that could be linked to the decennial censuses and the American Community Survey (ACS), as well as tax data from the SSA and the Internal Revenue Service (IRS).[4] Because there is a parent-child link of

---

[3] See https://www.census.gov/library/working-papers/2019/econ/adep-wp-dc-digitization-linkage.html.

[4] For Smeeding's full set of slides on this topic, see https://www.nationalacademies.org/event/09-27-2021/improving-consent-and-response-in-longitudinal-studies-of-aging-a-workshop.

SSNs through the IRS and since all children have had SSNs since 1987, all of these data can be linked inside an FSRDC and be protected. This opened up the possibility of linking the 1990 Census and earlier data and kick-started plans for the AOS.

Smeeding showed a summary slide of the current status of the AOS (Figure 5-3), which has three layers: Census data, administrative data, and potential linkages to different surveys. The Census data from 2000 and ACS data from 2008–2012 and 2013–2018 have already been linked. What is missing is in the red box of Figure 5-3: the 1960 to 1990 Censuses short and long forms. Some key variables, including income, education, occupation, work status, and family composition, are only available on the long form, which was administered to one in every six households. However, even the short form gives location, family, and occupation of parents.

In the second layer, Smeeding noted possible linkages to SSA earnings records, as well as program data from the Supplemental Nutrition Assistance Program, the Unemployment Insurance program, the Temporary Assistance for Needy Families program, Social Security programs, and Veterans' benefit programs. The IRS 1040 data from 1995 to 2012 are also available to link. Smeeding noted that the potential exists for linking with surveys of aging. He said that consent would be needed to link the survey to other sources, but much could be learned about the respondents with the high accuracy of Census linkages to the administrative data.

According to Smeeding, following the work and report of the Commission on Evidence Based Policymaking, attention has turned to a National Secure Data Service (NSDS), which would temporarily link these different data sources in a secure cloud environment for specific analyses, rather than creating a large linked dataset that would reside somewhere. He said NSDS could enable linkages to data from other agencies, such as the Centers for Disease Control and Prevention or other medical records and program data from the Veterans' Administration.

Smeeding said that consent would be needed to link to these data sources, as well as a personal identification key or SSN, after which the desired data could be extracted from the larger files and stored in a Research Data Center. He characterized this as the dream to which researchers are headed. He reiterated that links can be made from the 1850 to the 1940 Census, with the 1950 Census soon available. AOS can continue this linkage up through the 2010 and soon the 2020 census, so 170 years of American demographic history should be available.

Smeeding concluded with two discussion questions. First, he asked, "How can we interest survey responders to give broad consent to data linkage?" He suggested offering respondents a personal genealogy report. Respondents who are 70, 60, or older can be asked where they were living in 1950 or 1940, their parents' names, and their parents' location in 1940

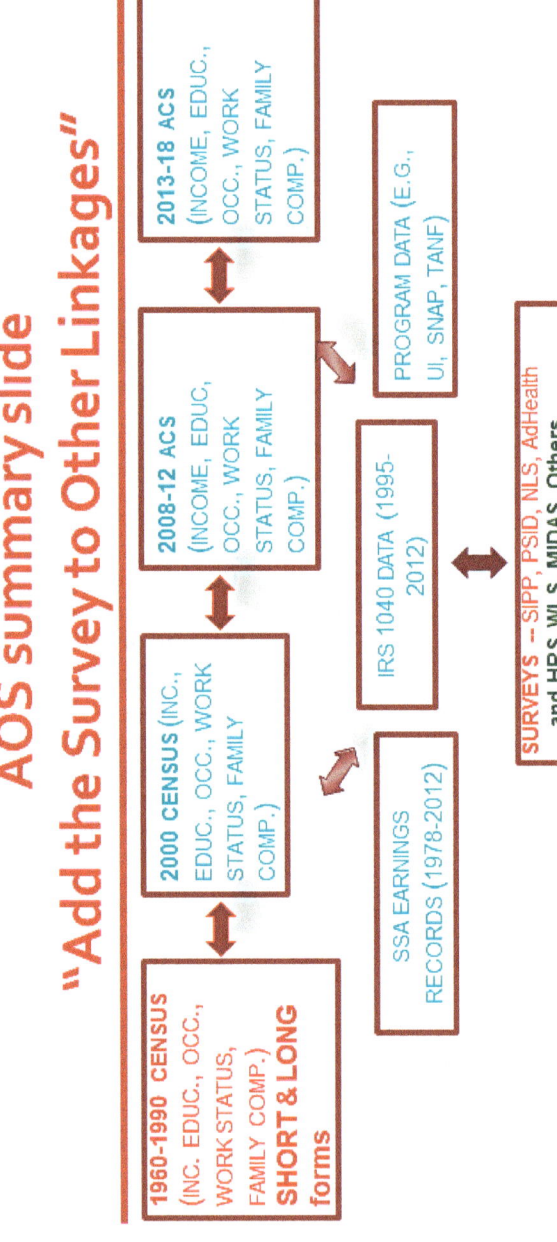

FIGURE 5-3 The American Opportunity Study backbone and opportunities for survey linkages.
SOURCE: Timothy Smeeding workshop presentation, September 28, 2021.

or 1950. That information can be used to link them back generation to generation using the Census link file.

Second, he asked, "What incentives can help respondents allow you to go forward, linking their records to those of their offspring?" The goal would be consent of the children of the survey respondents, who will be in some of the Censuses between 1950 and 1990, and be able to link to their Social Security, Census, Veterans, IRS, and other records. He said that these possibilities can enrich the current survey dataset by getting more data on the children or on the predecessors of the elderly.

Bias Propensity to Inform Responsive and Adaptive Survey Design in a Longitudinal Study

Andy Peytchev commented on the emergence of many interesting developments and innovations with longitudinal panels. He described what he characterized as an exciting study because its design is flexible and adaptable to other settings and demonstrates the reduction of bias, which is often difficult to do without an experimental design.

Peytchev defined responsive designs as a type of phased design in which different protocols are introduced in stages where researchers monitor different outcomes and obtain cost and error tradeoffs. By contrast, adaptive designs are different and come from a literature on clinical study designs. Adaptive designs tailor the protocols to particular sets of cases/individuals. He said that both of these designs come into play because the researcher can tailor phases of the design and target individual groups of cases.

Responsive and adaptive designs have been increasing in popularity because of increasing nonresponse, Peytchev said. They tend to be more advanced than normal survey designs, he explained, and require statistical models to target more expensive efforts to reduce error in the surveys without implementing a costly protocol for the full sample. The more information available for the models, the more effective they can be, at least theoretically.

Peytchev noted that longitudinal studies offer an opportunity to use these designs because of the availability of information on sample cases from prior waves or from the sampling frame. A variety of modeling approaches have been used, including machine learning approaches. He advocated taking a social science perspective and being careful and deliberate about what variables are used and what exactly is being modeled.

Peytchev described the way response propensity models have been used in surveys to reduce bias due to departures from probability-based designs and survey nonresponse. In this approach, one predicts the probability of being a respondent or nonrespondent using all the possible information that one has to predict how likely they are to participate. While machine learning methods are a good fit with this approach, he cautioned that implementation can be flawed when it becomes a blind pursuit of maximizing the prediction of whether a person would be a respondent with variables that are not associated with the survey variables of interest.

Propensity models can be used during data collection to identify nonrespondents for alternative treatment regimens or to reduce the risk of nonresponse bias, he continued. Some researchers have targeted the lowest response propensities, those who are the most difficult and necessary cases. Others have used response propensities at later stages in the data collection to identify high-propensity cases among the remaining nonrespondents.

Peytchev introduced the notion of bias propensity. Bias propensity is not simply maximizing the prediction of nonresponse, but including variables that are associated with the survey variables of interest or variables that are close approximations of the things that researchers want to measure as well as demographic characteristics, which are often related to many survey variables. He defined bias propensity as one minus the response propensity based on variables of substantive interest.

Peytchev described research using data from the 2013 Update of the High School Longitudinal Study of 2009. Ninth-graders were originally recruited in schools in 2009, and information on these students was available from multiple sources, including their baseline interviews, follow-up surveys, and some administrative data from the schools. Strengths of this study, he said, were that they had measures of nonresponse bias based on the three different sources of information; they created a simulated control condition using propensity scoring, so that a sample of cases did not receive the experimental treatment; and they evaluated survey outcomes before and after the intervention phase rather than after multiple additional follow-up phases.

Peytchev described the phased design of the study. In Phase 1, an email invitation and postal invitations were sent for a self-administered web survey, followed by telephone interviewers calling sampled members. In Phase 2, which was the focus of this research, a $5 prepaid incentive was offered to cases with the highest bias propensity who had not participated by the end of Phase 1. Additional phases included $15 and $25 promised incentives and abbreviated interviews, which were used as benchmarks to evaluate how well the intervention had worked.

In describing the results, Peytchev said the $5 prepaid incentive had an impact and resulted in a higher response rate. Bias propensity was estimated using a logistic regression model that had two vectors: one with demographic variables and one with substantive variables. To simulate the control condition, a logistic regression model with paradata was fit to data from cases that were not targeted in Phase 2, and used to estimate Phase 2 response propensities without the prepaid incentive for cases in the treatment group. He said that cases that were predicted to not have participated without the treatment were included in the control group.

Peytchev described the key results (Figure 5-4). The first yellow bar in the figure shows the average absolute bias of 3.6 percent, which was averaged across the multiple estimates from the prior round data, baseline interviews, and administrative data. This number represents a comparison of the estimate from the full sample to those who responded at the end of the main data collection (Phase 1). The second yellow bar (end of Phase 2 control) represents what the bias would have been if they had continued data collection without targeting sample cases with higher bias propensity: the bias would have remained essentially the same. However, the intervention in Phase 2 reduced the average absolute bias by about 1 percentage point, as seen in the third yellow bar (end of phase 2 treatment). He said that about one-quarter of the bias is being removed by this targeting based on predicted bias. The last yellow bar (with all follow-up phases) shows how effective all the other subsequent interventions were in reducing bias and that the average absolute bias drops down to about 1 percentage point.

Peytchev said that the fourth bar could be viewed as a gold standard, which is what the blue bars represent. The third blue bar shows that

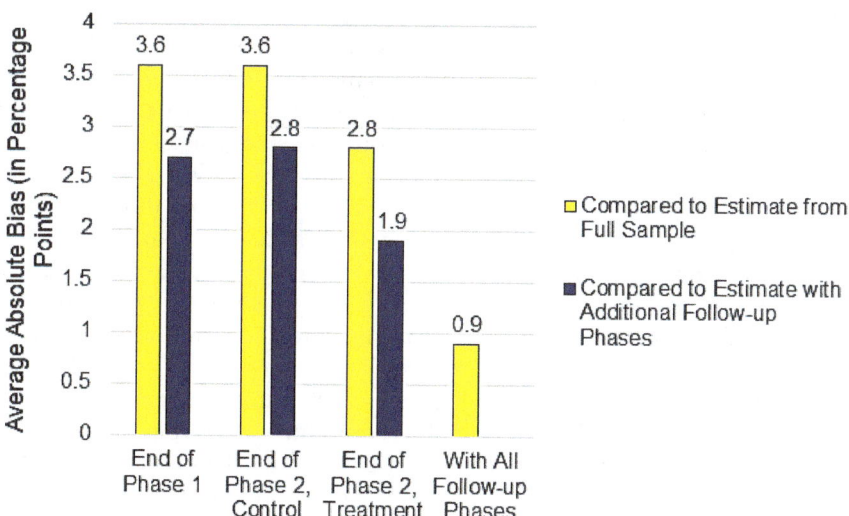

FIGURE 5-4 Average absolute bias for variables from a past round and from the sampling frame from the 2013 Update of the High School Longitudinal Study of 2009.
SOURCE: Andy Peytchev, workshop presentation, September 28, 2021, and Peytchev et al. (2020); reprinted with permission.

targeting cases based on bias propensity reduces the average absolute bias from 2.8 to 1.9. Using variables that came from the 2013 survey itself, so there is no assumption about lack of change over time, Peytchev showed that the pattern of results is essentially the same: average absolute bias decreased 0.7 percentage points with the intervention compared to the control condition.

Peytchev concluded by saying that the treatment condition was effective in reducing nonresponse bias compared to the control condition for most estimates, regardless of whether follow-up data, frame data, or baseline data were used. The treatment condition reduced the average absolute bias by approximately one percentage point, or roughly about one-quarter of the estimated bias. Similar reductions in average absolute bias reduction were achieved on the survey variables as well.

Discussion

Davern asked Phillips to start the discussion. Phillips noted that Jäckle's sample was of the entire adult population, with participants of varying ages, and asked about age effects in the results of the two different interventions she described as more or less important depending on the respondent's age. Jäckle replied that the consent research deliberately did not focus on social demographic predictors of consent because many previous studies have done so and found inconsistent results. She said that they have seen older participants are much more likely to make a trust-based decision than younger participants, and age effects could be studied further. In the study she described in this session, she pointed out younger groups are more likely to participate in studies involving mobile apps. However, she continued, whether or not people are already doing similar kinds of things for their own purposes is a bigger predictor than their social demographic characteristics. For example, if the respondent was already using a mobile app to check their accounts or bank, then they had a much higher probability of participating in the spending study than those who did not use an app, and this effect was larger than the age effects.

Phillips asked Smeeding about the match rates of Census panels to population surveys and what consent requirements are required to link a survey to link to these data in the FSRDCs. He also asked where researchers can access those data once matched. Smeeding referred to an article by Abramitzky et al. (2021) with information on the linkages, algorithms, and quality of the matching back to 1850. He noted that Steve Ruggles and Rob Warren, both at the University of Minnesota, pioneered the digitizing and matching of the Censuses that go back to 1850. Data linkage is the new science, he said, and, similar to addressing nonresponse in a survey through weighting, a nonmatch across administrative records or across long panels also needs to be addressed, which Abramitzky et al. (2021) discuss. In terms of consent, Smeeding suggested offering to provide respondents with Census information that would trace their genealogy as a motivating factor. The DCDL project he highlighted in his presentation provides more information on using data in the FSRDCs.

Davern posed a question to Smeeding from Robert Hummer about suggested language for consent to link to the AOS family of surveys. Davern further asked about the most critically important fields to collect in one's own survey to be able to successfully link. Smeeding suggested talking with Census Bureau staff and looking at the variables used to link the data from the Censuses. He noted Abramitzky et al. (2021) discussed the variables to use for the linkage, but added that asking such questions as "where did you live in 1950; what was your street address; what were your parents' names" could be useful. He also pointed out that use of administrative data is becoming much more common in the research literature, and about half of data-driven papers in the *American Economic Review* now use some sort of linked data. He is seeing increased interest and directs researchers to the experts who are creating and making available the linked data.

Phillips asked Peytchev the degree of nonresponse acceptable for some of the approaches he discussed. For example, he asked whether a study that had a 35 percent response rate could use Peytchev's approach to produce a representative sample, or would a higher response be needed to make those techniques feasible. Peytchev responded that a survey with a 35 percent response rate is a perfect case with a lot of potential for nonresponse bias. He said one could calculate it by multiplying the nonresponse rate times the difference between the respondents and nonrespondents on a survey variable, so a 35 percent response rate would be a multiplier of .65 for any differences that one has between the means. He noted in the 1980s and early 1990s, when face-to-face surveys had response rates in the 90 percent range, there was little concern for bias. Now, however, every survey is in the realm where nonresponse bias is a real threat.

Peytchev said that he tried to convey that it matters how resources and extra effort are spent to increase the response rate. Rather than spending across the full sample equally, he advocates using resources more strategically to deploy additional effort on the part of the sample that may be more biasing. He noted longitudinal studies can provide a lot of information to inform these designs. He added that the response propensity example is a relatively simple approach that does not require advanced modeling methods, but is more about carefully selecting variables to reduce bias.

6

Wrap-Up Discussion

The final session of the workshop was devoted to a panel discussion with members of the planning committee: Michael Davern, Jennifer Madans, Sunita Sah, and Vetta Sanders Thompson, along with John Phillips from the National Institute on Aging (NIA). As moderator of the discussion, Brian Harris-Kojetin began by asking the panelists what they saw as the take-home points from the sessions they chaired or from other sessions in the workshop. He also asked them what areas they thought NIA should prioritize for further research that would help advance some of the concerns and issues raised in the workshop.

TAKE-HOME POINTS AND RESEARCH PRIORITIES

Davern returned to his initial remarks that surveys are in crisis due to challenges related to nonresponse and nonresponse bias, as well as the global pandemic. He pointed out researchers are being forced to adapt their methodology for aging studies because that population is at high risk. Furthermore, there are risks with some of the methods currently used to collect important data, such as physical measures or biomeasures. Moving forward, he urged asking what is missing from the stories about the current crisis in survey response. Every story leaves out important factors and perspectives that are not represented, he said. He asked workshop participants to consider what is missing or not being focused on that could be essential to resolve this crisis with surveys.

Maintaining Contact Over Time

Many of the longitudinal studies discussed at the workshop represented initial investments from NIA or other federal agencies, Davern continued, and 20 or 30 years later, the studies are still contacting the same people. Yet over the life of a study, contact or engagement with respondents is not maintained because of insufficient funding. He urged thinking about how to centralize some kind of repository to maintain contact with respondents in important data collections even if there is not funding for data collection some years. Failing to maintain contact and engagement is a lost opportunity for the future, he observed, and keeping electronic contact through email, social media, and other available tools is a valuable idea that came up during the workshop.

For research priorities, Davern suggested an engagement strategy for trying to stay in touch with and maintain contact information over time with participants in large surveys, even when there might not be funding for a regular data collection. He stressed the importance of being able to recontact them effectively later if there is funding or interest in follow-on studies with that group of people.

Geographic Differences

Thompson picked up on Davern's comment on variables and factors that no one had discussed during the workshop. She noted that no one talked about geographic differences, and that she suspects that geographic differences are likely, particularly for some minority populations simply because of their concentration and relationship in the context given their numbers and political positioning, their reaction to authority and government, and other factors. She also noted that education in the context of aging relates to the cognitive capacity to consent and is important to consider.

Overall, Thompson said she heard consensus on what to do to successfully recruit and get people to participate, especially in person. However, shifting to the web where those social dynamics that drive people to agree are absent poses more problems, she observed. She was also surprised about the consistency in the way presenters talked about their ability to identify the resources and the techniques necessary to convert refusals and to build up a response rate even on the web.

Ethical Considerations in Consent

Thompson added that what struck her is the need to shift focus, because the ethical considerations and the complexities discussed lead her to wonder about the need to think about stakeholders differently. She referred to a question posed by Christine Grady: What gets people to feel like they will be making an important contribution that is meaningful to society and thus something that they really want to do as opposed to us just trying to figure out how to get people to say yes? Thompson added that as long as the goal is simply to get people to say yes, investigators will be less personal and more reliant on technologies that remove an in-person social dynamic, and the more surveys are going to suffer. People may avoid doing surveys because they are so prevalent. Although they do make a distinction between surveys that are very important to health and well-being compared to many other kinds, they need to hear the story in a way that is appealing to them, she said. She urged putting more resources into understanding the "whys" of various stakeholder groups, then communicating more effectively whether via email, text, or telephone. Perhaps less communication will suffice, she said, and people might be more motivated over a sustained time period without additional incentives.

Understanding Why People Consent

From her perspective of an organizational psychologist, Sah said she picked up on Thompson's comments on understanding the "why" of participation. She noted that consent varies between people as well as within the same person over time. At one particular point of time, they may say yes; at another point of time, they may say no or vice versa. Understanding why is hugely important to figure out, she emphasized.

Sah noted that collecting data online will become more important and pointed to the tension about giving away personal data too freely online. People will agree to many things online and give personal data away, but they also worry about how much data they are giving away. She asked, "What is it that people want to tell us and how could that help us in collecting the data that is also essential?" She also described how some people say they would like to help and will participate, but then do not. Sah asked what to do to close the gap between people's statements and actual follow-through and to understand why the gap is happening at that particular stage.

In terms of research priorities, Sah suggested trying to understand the psychological processes of why people consent, in what situations, what factors influence their consent, and what factors influence their retention is important. Trust is an important factor, she said, and highlighted the discussion on the role of online influencers, friends, and family in building trust. Every brand has a different level of trust and will bring in different people and different voices, she observed. She considers this is an important area of research because personalized consent is going to be difficult, and the way to reach more people will be through brands and influencers. Areas for research include how to build a brand that is trusted to conduct these types of surveys and with whom to partner, Sah said.

Improving Initial Response Rates

Madans commented she was probably not as optimistic as other presenters and committee members. She identified two streams in the presentations: one approach is to improve response overall and keep people in surveys, and the second is to reduce bias after the fact. She commented most researchers are doing all the obvious things to get the highest response rates, but there is no silver bullet. People vary in their preferences. Targeting approaches to each respondent to appeal to them and their decision to consent could be done, but she recognized that it is not feasible on a large scale.

To Madans, getting people in the beginning of longitudinal surveys is critical. Response rates are going down to a point where there are huge risks of nonresponse bias. Madans asked if something structural could be done rather than trying to target individual approaches for specific groups of respondents. She noted that there is no brand for the federal statistical system and asked how a potential respondent could distinguish the good surveys from the bad ones. She urged reeducating the public writ large, rather than individual survey respondents, about the use and benefits of surveys for the public good. Madans said that approach would not be easy or extremely successful, but neither is trying to tailor information to each individual respondent.

Reducing Bias

Madans then turned to the approach of addressing bias reduction after the fact, noting that it is still necessary to get a certain level of response in order to conduct bias reduction. She asked what can be done to ameliorate the fact that one no longer has a representative sample, and how to evaluate if big groups of people have been missed. She referred to the design discussed by Andy Peytchev. It is difficult to bring more people into the sample who have different experiences or ideas that are not related to demographics, she commented.

Madans said she sees opportunities with using linked data more in survey design as opposed to only getting additional information. This would present a consent issue, she acknowledged, and also is affected by the way the data system in the United States works with many different data owners. She urged doing everything possible to reduce risk for disclosure and make people more comfortable with data linkage, and there is a lot of interest in doing that now. Madans concluded by noting that scientific surveys are costly and resources are limited. She asked how to prioritize what is most needed given limited resources so as to maximize the overall benefit.

In terms of research priorities, Madans said that research on bias reduction after data collection is important, but that it should be included in the survey design so that information is obtained that can be used to reduce bias after collection. She said that if there are auxiliary data that might be useful for bias reduction, one needs to make sure one collects the data in the survey so that the auxiliary data can be used effectively.

DISCUSSION OF ADDITIONAL PRIORITIES FOR FUTURE RESEARCH

Coordinating Research Across Studies

Madans also noted that many surveys include experiments, but there is pressure not to use sample persons in a way that would affect the substantive analyses of the survey. As a result the experiments are limited and do not permit looking at important interaction effects. She suggested NIA consider funding innovation panels to invest in research that is best done in conjunction with an ongoing survey without being concerned about losing cases. It would be especially useful to do coordinated research across multiple surveys that are looking at the same experimental conditions so that there is more power to look at experimental effects and interactions of different surveys and conditions, which would help identify innovations for improving the methodology for everybody, Madans suggested.

Increasing Research Literacy

Thompson singled out consent for biological samples as a pain point and pointed to discussion about what people understand even when they consent. She added she has been thinking about this in the context of vaccine hesitancy. What people know about biology, science, health, and research affects their responses. She suggested working with communication and education systems to better understand people's needs to assist agencies working to promote health and well-being. Thompson noted that her organization has done work around increasing research literacy and has seen how enthusiastic people become about research, which makes a difference in their participation.

Linking to Administrative Records

Davern mentioned the missingness that happens when surveys and administrative records are linked. He said it would be good to think about how to create inferential tools like weights or other tools to generalize to a population and understand the inferential population of linked cases in order to conduct important health and aging research on those linked datasets. He said understanding the inferences and the limitations of the inferences using joint data products is a good use of resources.

Davern expressed interest in Timothy Smeeding's presentation, but noted its focus on government data. In the commercial space, Davern said, the rules of data governance are different. He said that trying to work with commercial health care providers to get health care, medical record, laboratory, or payment information can be difficult but also worth the effort. Tools mentioned by Lisa Mirel around the use of Privacy Protected Record Linkage are being used by commercial entities to link data, he said, and commented it is a fascinating area to explore. He also suggested engaging with commercial enterprises to ensure continuity because they can terminate access to their data at any given time. They could feel threatened by the potential release of proprietary information or research studies that could help their competitors by divulging something about their patient population, he commented.

Smeeding agreed that commercial data are difficult because companies want to keep some things secret, and they can make money off their data. He endorsed the idea of using surveys to link to government records, adding that maintaining contact with people who are otherwise difficult to locate would be an amazing possibility. Maintaining contact is important, and he recalled the contribution of Tecla Loup, a former staff member of the Panel Study of Income, who "knew everyone and sent them a Christmas card every year." He emphasized that using administrative and survey data together strengthens and improves surveys. Surveys provide important information that administrative records cannot and serve as the "glue between the bricks from the administrative data," he commented.

Issues of Ethical Consent and Privacy Over Time

Davern raised another issue about what happens ethically in supporting the research with respect to consent and records after a participant dies. He noted that the rules for human subjects no longer apply, and there is a lot of variability in how this is handled. The Census statute is very clear about the 72-year rule for protecting confidentiality, but he asked about long-term studies. He said he foresees many possibilities in the next 10, 20, or 30 years for how to reuse some of those data to provide information about the life course of the people and those cohorts.

Smeeding noted that linked Census data have been used to look at African American mobility over time, and noted other opportunities to use those data to address important questions. Thompson said that she spent a lot of time talking to people in the community about the level of protection of their privacy and the fact that they have to give consent for some of these linkages because they have real fears, particularly for government data. She advised being very thoughtful in proceeding with these linkages and how the linkages are explained to the public; otherwise, people will refuse to participate from the beginning. She underscored the need to respect people's right to make the decisions themselves, especially those whose rights have been taken in the past. Smeeding agreed with the importance to attend to these issues and clarified that the paper on mobility he mentioned uses data from 1850 to 1940. Phillips commented while he is enthusiastic about linking to Census data, it will not be easy. He anticipates consent will be needed not just for the federal agencies to link the data, but also that Institutional Review Boards (IRBs) will have requirements for the reasons that Thompson raised.

Madans agreed with Thompson, and noted that the 2020 decennial Census devoted considerable time and money on messaging how the data are completely protected and confidential. She observed that very few people know the protection ends after 72 years, and that many other federal laws do not have end dates. She urged care and balance in moving science forward with people's ideas and views of their rights regarding their information. To maintain trust, scientists should not be trying to convince people to do something they do not want to do, but instead building trust in ethical ways. Echoing Thompson and Sah, she stressed figuring out what is really important to people, finding a common thread to obtain participation and trust from a good majority of people, and then taking care to maintain that trust.

Sah commented that valid consent is key to building trust and retaining participants. She noted that insinuation anxiety is probably more relevant to vulnerable populations, and the social pressure to get consent needs to be reduced. For ongoing consent, she advised making participation more attractive and decreasing the cost of participation by making it more convenient, less burdensome, and by providing incentives or clear benefits so respondents see their contributions to science and society.

NIA PERSPECTIVES ON THE WORKSHOP

Harris-Kojetin turned to Phillips for his observations and questions for the panel. Phillips commented on the different ways the various longitudinal aging studies are attempting to deal with the same issues. He noted that these findings and tests are often not published or widely circulated, and that sharing this information is a priority to help all the surveys. Pointing to the discussion on the limitations on what some studies may do as a result of differences between IRBs, he said he was not sure how to address this other than greater sharing of protocols and practices across studies.

Referring to the several presentations about administrative data, including those by Andy Peytchev and Joe Sakshaug, Phillips questioned what the administrative data backbone for aging studies should be and what minimum data are necessary to use the statistical techniques presented to deal with nonresponse bias. He also identified a theme across several presentations that a combination of awareness and engagement across time seems to keep people engaged in studies. He added that when people are more aware of or had experience in health studies, they are less likely to be worried about consenting for a new one. He suggested building on this awareness, and that making the scientific and research process better understood may inherently improve people's willingness to participate. He asked the group to consider how to make people more aware of science findings and the impact on science from these studies that might help improve participation.

Phillips said he is excited about the possibilities of self-administered biospecimen collections to get more participation in an inexpensive way. He expressed interest in hearing results on the use of the BioBox, and he hypothesized that some participants may be more willing to do some of the tasks if they have someone else present to help or participate.

Phillips closed by expressing appreciation to the presenters, the committee organizing the workshop, and all the participants. Harris-Kojetin echoed Phillips's comments and also thanked the National Institute of Aging for sponsoring the workshop.

References

Abramitzky, R., Boustan, L., Eriksson, K., Feigenbaum, J., and Pérez, S. (2021). Automated linking of historical data. *Journal of Economic Literature, 59*(3), 865–918. Available: https://doi.org/10.1257/jel.20201599.

Biemer, P., Harris, K.M., Halpern, C., Burke, B., and Liao, D. (Forthcoming). Transitioning a panel survey from in-person to predominantly web data collection: Results and lessons learned. *Journal of the Royal Statistical Society*, forthcoming special issue on The Future of Online Data Collection in Social Surveys.

Burton, J., Couper, M.P., Crossley, T.F., Jäckle, A., and Walzenbach, S. (2021). How Do Survey Respondents Decide Whether to Consent to Data Linkage? *Understanding Society Working Paper 2021-05*. Colchester: University of Essex. Available: https://www.understandingsociety.ac.uk/research/publications/547074.

Büttner, T.J.M., Sakshaug, J.W., and Vicari, B. 2021. Evaluating the utility of linked administrative data for nonresponse bias adjustment in a piggyback longitudinal survey. *Journal of Official Statistics, 37*(4), 837–864. https://doi.org/10.2478/jos-2021-0037.

Grusky, D.B., Smeeding, T.M, and Snipp, C.M. (2015). A New Infrastructure for Monitoring Social Mobility in the United States. *Annals of the American Academy of Political and Social Science, 657*(1): 63–82.

Grusky, D.B., Hout, M., Smeeding, T.M., & Snipp, C.M. (2019). The American Opportunity Study: A New Infrastructure for Monitoring Outcomes, Evaluating Policy, and Advancing Basic Science. *RSF: The Russell Sage Foundation Journal of the Social Sciences, 5*(2), 20–39. https://doi.org/10.7758/rsf.2019.5.2.02

Harris, K.M., Halpern, C.T., Biemer, P., Liao, D., and Dean, S.C. (2019). Sampling and mixed-mode survey design. Add Health Wave V Documentation. Available: https://addhealth.cpc.unc.edu/wp-content/uploads/docs/user_guides/Add-Health-Wave-V-Sampling-and-Mixed-Mode-Survey-Design_doi.pdf.

Lidz, C.W., Appelbaum, P.S., and Meisel, A. (1988). Two models of implementing informed consent. *Archives of Internal Medicine, 148*(6), 1385–1389.

Miller, F.G., and Wertheimer, A. (2010). Preface to a theory of consent transactions: Beyond valid consent. *The Ethics of Consent: Theory and Practice*, 79–105.

Peytchev, A., Pratt, D., and Duprey, M. (2022). Responsive and adaptive survey design: Use of bias propensity during data collection to reduce nonresponse bias. *Journal of Survey Statistics and Methodology*, 10(1), 131–148.

Radler, B.T., and Ryff, C.D. (2010). Who participates? Accounting for longitudinal retention in the MIDUS national study of health and well-being. *Journal of Aging and Health*, 22, 307–331.

Sakshaug, J.W., and Huber, M. (2016). An evaluation of panel nonresponse and linkage consent bias in a survey of employees in Germany. *Journal of Survey Statistics and Methodology*, 4(1), 71–93.

Sakshaug, J.W., and Kreuter, F. (2012). Assessing the Magnitude of Non-Consent Biases in Linked Survey and Administrative Data. *Survey Research Methods*, 6(2), 113–122.

Silverwood, R.J., Calderwood, L., Sakshaug, J.W., and Ploubidis, G.B. (2020). A Data Driven Approach to Understanding and Handling Non-Response in the Next Steps Cohort. CLS Working Paper 2020/5. London: UCL Centre for Longitudinal Studies. Available: https://cls.ucl.ac.uk/wp-content/uploads/2020/04/CLS-working-paper-2020-5-A-data-driven-approach-to-understanding-and-handling-non-response-in-the-Next-Steps-cohort.pdf.

Song, J., Radler, B.T., Lachman, M.E., Mailick, M.R., Yajuan, S., and Ryff, C.D. (2021). Who returns? Understanding varieties of longitudinal participation in MIDUS. *Journal of Aging and Health*, 33, 896–907. Available: https://journals.sagepub.com/doi/pdf/10.1177/08982643211018552.

Ward, Z. (2021). Intergenerational Mobility in American History: Accounting for Race and Measurement Error. NBER Working Paper Series. Available: https://www.nber.org/system/files/working_papers/w29256/w29256.pdf.

Appendix A

Public Meeting Agenda

IMPROVING CONSENT AND RESPONSE IN LONGITUDINAL STUDIES OF AGING: A WORKSHOP[1]

September 27–28, 2021

12:00   Welcome and Introduction
Brian Harris-Kojetin, CNSTAT
John Phillips, National Institute on Aging

Goals of the Workshop
Michael Davern, NORC at the University of Chicago, *Planning Committee Chair*

BACKGROUND AND CONTEXT

12:15   Opportunities and Challenges with Response and Consent in Longitudinal Surveys on Aging
Chair: **Vetta L. Sanders Thompson,** Washington University in St. Louis

---

[1] Presenters' slides and videos of the entire workshop are available at https://www.nationalacademies.org/event/09-27-2021/improving-consent-and-response-in-longitudinal-studies-of-aging-a-workshop.

Participants:
Carol Ryff, University of Wisconsin
Linda Waite, University of Chicago
Bob Hummer, University of North Carolina, Chapel Hill
David Weir, University of Michigan

1:20 Identifying and Reducing Selection Bias
Chair: Jennifer H. Madans, retired, National Center for Health Statistics
Participants:
Joe Sakshaug, University of Mannheim
Debra Reed Gillette, Centers for Medicare and Medicaid Services
Andy Peytchev, RTI International

2:15 Break

PARTICIPATION

2:30 Maximizing Respondent Retention
Chair: Michael Davern, NORC at the University of Chicago
Participants:
Nicole Watson, University of Melbourne
Eric Grodsky, University of Wisconsin, and Rachel Canas, NORC at the University of Chicago
Pam Herd, Georgetown University

DATA LINKAGE

3:30 Challenges to Connecting Data across Agencies
Chair: Jennifer H. Madans, retired, National Center for Health Statistics
Participants:
Beth Virnig, University of Minnesota
Lisa Mirel, National Center for Health Statistics

4:30 Day One Wrap-Up
Michael Davern, NORC at the University of Chicago

4:45 Adjourn

DAY 2
TUESDAY SEPTEMBER 28, 2021

12:00 Intro and Recap of Day One
Michael Davern, NORC at the University of Chicago, *Planning Committee Chair*

INFORMED CONSENT

12:10 The Complexity of Informed Consent
Chair: **Vetta L. Sanders Thompson,** Washington University in St. Louis
Participants:
    Annette Jäckle, University of Essex
    Katie O'Doherty, NORC at the University of Chicago
    Christine Grady, National Institutes of Health

1:05 Ethical Considerations for Obtaining Informed Consent
Chair: **Vetta L. Sanders Thompson,** Washington University in St. Louis
Participants:
    Stephanie Solomon Cargill, St. Louis University
    Emily Largent, University of Pennsylvania
    Sunita Sah, University of Cambridge and Cornell University

2:00 Break

PARTICIPATION

2:15 Participant Engagement: Insights from Behavioral Science Research
Chair: **Sunita Sah,** University of Cambridge and Cornell University
Participants:
    Bettina Drake, Washington University School of Medicine in St. Louis
    Amelia Burke-Garcia, NORC at the University of Chicago

INNOVATION

3:15   Looking Ahead: Applying Innovative Strategies to Improve Consent and Response
Chair: **Michael Davern,** NORC at the University of Chicago
Participants:
     Annette Jäckle, University of Essex
     Timothy Smeeding, University of Wisconsin
     Andy Peytchev, RTI International

4:15   Wrap-Up Discussion
Chair: **Brian Harris-Kojetin,** CNSTAT
Participants:
     John Phillips, National Institute on Aging
     Michael Davern, NORC at the University of Chicago
     Jennifer H. Madans, retired, National Center for Health Statistics
     Sunita Sah, University of Cambridge and Cornell University
     Vetta L. Sanders Thompson, Washington University in St. Louis

5:00   Adjourn

Appendix B

Committee and Speaker Biosketches

AMELIA BURKE-GARCIA is a seasoned health communications professional with nearly 20 years of experience in health communication program planning, implementation, and evaluation, with specific expertise in developing and evaluating digital health communications campaigns and intervention studies. Over the course of her career, Burke-Garcia has spearheaded innovative communication programs and studies on a variety of health topics. Examples include investigating perspectives and motivations of non-vaccinating online influencers, designing a targeted social media intervention with "mommy bloggers" to help social media users lower their risk for breast cancer, and leveraging MeetUp groups and the Waze mobile application to move people to action around flu vaccination and HIV testing, respectively. Most recently, she acted as director for the award-winning *How Right Now/Que Hacer Ahora* campaign, which is aimed at increasing people's ability to cope and be resilient amidst the COVID-19 pandemic. She is also conducting three studies that examine perceptions and beliefs related to the COVID vaccine among hard-to-reach populations. She is the author of the book *Influencing Health: A Comprehensive Guide to Working with Online Influencers* and has been named to VeryWellHealth.com's list of 10 Modern Female Innovators Shaking Up Health Care.

RACHEL CANAS is a senior research director in the Health Sciences Department at NORC at the University of Chicago. She currently serves as the assistant project director for the High School & Beyond (HS&B) Follow Up study, a longitudinal, multimode (web, Computer Assisted Telephone Interview, paper) study looking at the intersection of health, cognition, and education. She also serves as a lead project manager for the Survey of Women multimode data collection, an address-based longitudinal study collecting sensitive health measures via web and mail surveys. Her primary expertise is with managing data collection efforts for large-scale, multimode studies. Her work spans questionnaire development, design of data collection technical systems, management of multimode data collection operations, and training of interviewers and locators. Prior to NORC, she managed multiple efforts related to questionnaire and instrument development across single-mode and multimode data collections at the University of Michigan Survey Research Operations. She has an M.S. in survey and data science from the University of Michigan.

STEPHANIE SOLOMON CARGILL is associate professor of health care ethics at Saint Louis University, with a focus on research ethics. Solomon Cargill's empirical and theoretical research explores the ethical and policy issues that face research review boards like Institutional Review Boards (IRBs) and community advisory boards, as well as more specific issues around informed consent and research with vulnerable individuals and communities. She is the chair of Castle IRB, a private IRB that specializes in reviewing gene and cell therapy research, and she sits on Saint Louis University's IRB. She develops and implements curricula in research ethics, public health ethics, and responsible conduct of research for graduate students, medical students, and researchers.

MICK P. COUPER *(Steering Committee Member)* is a research professor in the Survey Research Center Institute for Social Research at the University of Michigan. He has been doing surveys and research on surveys for over 30 years. He is the author of *Designing Effective Web Surveys* and co-author of *The Science of Web Surveys, Nonresponse in Household Interview Surveys,* and *Survey Methodology.* He has published widely on survey methodology in a variety of journals. His research focuses on the application of technology to the survey process, the design of computer-assisted surveys, and the data collection process, including issues of coverage, nonresponse, and measurement. He has also conducted research on consent to biomeasures and administrative record linkage. He holds a Ph.D. in sociology from Rhodes University, an M.A. in applied social research from the University of Michigan, and an M.Soc.Sc. from the University of Cape Town.

MICHAEL DAVERN *(Steering Committee Chair)* is senior vice president and director of the Public Health Research Department at NORC at the University of Chicago. His work focuses on survey research, public health data, linking surveys with administrative data, and Census Bureau data, as well as the use of these data for policy research simulation and evaluation. Previously, at the University of Minnesota, he was an assistant professor of health policy and management, research director of the State Health Access Data Assistance Center, and co-director of the State Research Data Center. He also previously served as a statistician for the Labor Force and Transfer Programs Statistics Branch of the U.S. Census Bureau. A major focus of his work has involved applying state-level data to health policy issues and helping states monitor trends in health insurance coverage rates. He has an M.A. in sociology from Colorado State University and a Ph.D. in sociology from the University of Notre Dame.

BETTINA DRAKE is professor of surgery at Washington University School of Medicine in the Division of Public Health Sciences and associate director of community outreach and engagement at Siteman Cancer Center. Drake is a cancer epidemiologist and health disparities researcher with expertise in community-based research. Her research focuses on identifying preventive strategies to reduce disparities. The objectives of her research program are (1) to utilize community-based approaches to design, implement, and disseminate research information; (2) to promote education and awareness of research and research participation in minority communities; and (3) to identify the modifiable and nonmodifiable risk factors for cancer and other chronic diseases as well as the at-risk groups for these factors. The combination of her community-based and epidemiology expertise strengthens the effectiveness of her leadership for this component. She builds on the synergy between her community-engaged work and cancer epidemiology research to reduce health disparities and promote health equity.

CHRISTINE GRADY is a nurse-bioethicist, senior investigator, and chief of the Department of Bioethics at the National Institutes of Health Clinical Center. Her research focuses on clinical research ethics, including informed consent, vulnerability, study design, recruitment, international research ethics, and ethical issues faced by nurses and other health care providers. Grady has authored more than 200 papers in the biomedical and bioethics literature and authored or edited several books, including *The Oxford Textbook of Clinical Research Ethics*. She is an elected fellow of the Hastings Center and the American Academy of Nursing, a research fellow at Kennedy Institute of Ethics, and an elected member of the National Academy of Medicine. Grady holds a B.S. in nursing and biology from Georgetown University, M.S.N. in community health nursing from Boston College, and Ph.D. in philosophy from Georgetown University.

ERIC GRODSKY is professor of sociology and educational policy studies at the University of Wisconsin-Madison and co-principal investigator of High School & Beyond (HS&B). In addition to his work with HS&B, Grodsky co-directs the Madison Education Partnership, a research-practice partnership between the Wisconsin Center for Education Research and the Madison Metropolitan School District, and leads several projects with Wisconsin's state department of education. Grodsky has written on inequality in early childhood and higher education, educational gradients in morbidity and mortality, and social stratification over the life course more broadly. His work has appeared in the *American Journal of Sociology*, *American Sociological Review*, *Social Forces*, and *Sociology of Education*, among other venues.

PAMELA HERD is a professor in the McCourt School of Public Policy at Georgetown University and a principal investigator (PI) of the Wisconsin Longitudinal Study (2010-present). Her research focuses on health (especially biodemography), aging, stratification, and policy, with additional expertise in survey methods. She is a PI (with Sanjay Asthana) on a data collection project that is tracking dementia in the Wisconsin Longitudinal Study. She is also a member of the PI team for the General Social Survey. She is currently the NIH-appointed chair of the Data Monitoring Committee for the National Longitudinal Study of Adolescent to Adult Health (Add Health). Her research and data collection interests focus on relationships between social conditions and biological processes and outcomes, with particular interests in the relationships between social environments and biological outcomes. Her work has appeared in publications such as the *American Sociological Review*, *Proceedings of the National Academy of Sciences*, and *Nature Genetics*.

ROBERT A. HUMMER is the Howard W. Odum Distinguished Professor of Sociology and fellow of the Carolina Population Center at the University of North Carolina at Chapel Hill. Hummer is also currently serving as the president of the Population Association of America. His research program is focused on the accurate description and more complete understanding of population health patterns and trends in the United States. He is currently serving as director of the National Longitudinal Study of Adolescent to Adult Health (Add Health), which is funded by the National Institute on Aging and five co-funding institutes/offices. Over his career, he has published more than 150 journal articles and book chapters, with attention to health disparities both during infancy/childhood as well as across the adult life course. He is also co-author of *Population Health in America*.

ANNETTE JÄCKLE is professor for survey methodology at the Institute for Social Research (University of Essex, UK) and associate director for Innovations in Understanding Society. Current research projects focus on methods for event-triggered data collection, collecting informed consents for data linkage, and using mobile apps for data collection.

EMILY LARGENT is the Emanuel and Robert Hart Assistant Professor of Medical Ethics and Health Policy at the University of Pennsylvania. She holds a secondary appointment at Penn Law. Her work explores ethical and regulatory aspects of human subjects research and the translation of research findings into care, with a particular focus on Alzheimer's disease. In 2020, she was named a Greenwall Faculty Scholar; her faculty scholar project, "Autonomy on the Precipice of Cognitive Decline," seeks to understand how the evolving understanding of Alzheimer's disease affects patients and their families. She received her Ph.D. in health policy, with a concentration in ethics, from Harvard University and her J.D. from Harvard Law School. She was previously a fellow in the Department of Bioethics at the National Institutes of Health and clerked for Chief Judge Jeffrey Howard of the United States Court of Appeals for the First Circuit.

JENNIFER H. MADANS *(Steering Committee Member)* recently retired from the National Center for Health Statistics (NCHS), serving most recently as the center's associate director for science, acting director, and acting deputy director. She was responsible for the overall plan and development of NCHS's data collection and analysis programs. Her research has focused on efforts on data collection methodology and the measurement of health and functioning. She is a founding member and served as chair of the steering committees for three United Nations–sponsored initiatives to develop internationally comparable measures of disability and health, including the Washington Group on Disability Statistics, a city group under the auspices of the UN Statistical Commission making extensive contributions in all aspects of disability data collection internationally and in the United States. She is an elected fellow of the American Statistical Association, an elected member of the International Statistical Institute, and served as a vice president of the International Association of Official Statistics. She has a B.A. degree from Bard College and M.A. and Ph.D. degrees in sociology from the University of Michigan.

LISA MIREL is the chief of the Data Linkage Methodology and Analysis Branch in the Division of Analysis and Epidemiology at the National Center for Health Statistics (NCHS), Centers for Disease Control and Prevention. She directs the NCHS Data Linkage program, leading agency efforts to integrate NCHS data collection systems with external sources of health-related administrative data, to both expand the analytic potential of NCHS data and to develop innovative data resources that better inform public health policy and fill critical information gaps. She also oversees the development and implementation of state-of-the-art data linkage methodologies and data quality assessment tools. Her work has focused primarily on integrating multiple sources of data through data linkage and advising on survey design and estimation techniques for large-scale national health surveys. She received her M.S. in biostatistics from the University of Michigan's School of Public Health.

KATIE O'DOHERTY is a senior research director in the Health Sciences Department at NORC at the University of Chicago. Her expertise is in managing complex data collection projects that integrate biomeasure collection and cognitive assessments into survey research, including NIH projects such as the National Social Life, Health and Aging Project, the Abecedarian Project at Midlife, and High School and Beyond.

ANDY PEYTCHEV is a senior survey methodologist and fellow at RTI. He leads the design of large-scale surveys and principal investigator (PI)-initiated research, and is the RTI PI for the National Survey of Family Growth. His research interests include study designs that minimize survey error with particular emphasis on nonresponse and measurement error. Peytchev's recent work includes the evaluation of split questionnaire design, development of adaptive and responsive survey designs, implementation of multimode and multiphase data collection, augmentation of survey samples with other data, and synthetic data.

JOHN W. R. PHILLIPS serves as chief of the Population and Social Processes Branch of the Division of Behavioral and Social Research (BSR) in the National Institute on Aging (NIA). During a career spanning over 20 years, he has worked to produce research and data resources on aging-related topics. Prior to joining BSR, he was associate commissioner for research, evaluation, and statistics at the U.S. Social Security Administration (SSA). He previously served in other research roles in the federal government, including health scientist administrator for NIA, as well as research economist and director of the Office of Policy Research at SSA. His research has examined aging issues ranging from retirement security, intergenerational transfers, and distributional effects of retirement and disability programs. His current portfolio at NIA focuses on the economics of aging and the development of international comparators to the U.S. Health and Retirement Study to support aging research. He received a Ph.D. in economics from Syracuse University.

DEBRA REED-GILLETTE is currently director of the Survey Management and Analytics Group within the Office of Enterprise Data and Analytics of the Centers for Medicare & Medicaid Services. She has more than 30 years of experience in federal health surveys with the Centers for Disease Control and Prevention, including the National Health Interview Survey and the National Health and Nutrition Examination Survey. Additionally, she served as a subject matter expert for the Oregon Health Study, the first New York City Health and Nutrition Examination Survey, the Canadian Health Measures Study, Survey of the Health of Wisconsin, and the National Children's Study. Her expertise is in public health informatics focusing on public health-related data collection systems and data dissemination.

CAROL D. RYFF is director of the Institute on Aging and Hilldale Professor of Psychology at the University of Wisconsin-Madison. She studies how psychological well-being varies by age, gender, educational status, cultural context, and how it matters for diverse aspects of health including disease outcomes, length of life, physiological regulation, and neural circuitry. Her model of well-being is widely used around the world, with the assessment scales translated to more than 40 languages. Ryff is principal investigator of the MIDUS (Midlife in the U.S.) longitudinal study and its sister study in Japan, MIDJA (Midlife in Japan), for which she received an NIH Merit Award. Her scientific contributions (270+ publications) have been recognized with the Baltes Distinguished Research Award and the Mentoring Award from Division 20 of the American Psychological Association, Positive Health Award from the International Network of Positive Psychology, Murray Award from the Society of Personality and Social Psychology, Lifetime Achievement Award from the International Network for Personal Meaning, and Matilda White Riley Award from the National Institute on Aging.

SUNITA SAH *(Steering Committee Member)* is a physician turned professor and organizational psychologist at Cornell University and an honorary fellow at the University of Cambridge. She teaches leadership, negotiations, and critical thinking. Her research expertise is in conflicts of interest, disclosure, influence, consent, compliance, and trust. Sah is the director of academic leadership at Cornell University. She served as a commissioner on the National Commission of Forensic Science and on the Human Factors Committee for the National Institute of Science and Technology Forensic Science Standards Board. She is currently on the scientific advisory board of the Behavioral Economics in Health Network, an officer of the International Behavioural Public Policy Association, a fellow of the Society of Personality and Social Psychology, and on the editorial board of *Behavioural Public Policy*. She has won best paper and scholar awards from a number of U.S. and UK organizations. Prior to Cornell University, Sah was the KPMG Professor of Management Studies at the University of Cambridge, and earlier held academic positions at Georgetown, Duke, Russell Sage, and Harvard

Universities. Before entering academia, she worked as a medical doctor for the UK National Health Service. Sah holds a Ph.D. and M.S. in organizational behavior from Carnegie Mellon University, M.B.A. from London Business School, an M.B. Ch.B. in medicine and surgery and a B.Sc. (Hons) in psychology from the University of Edinburgh.

JOE SAKSHAUG is distinguished researcher at the German Institute for Employment Research, professor of statistics at the Ludwig Maximilian University of Munich, and honorary professor in the school of social sciences at the University of Mannheim. He also teaches in the International Program in Survey and Data Science. He is well known for his contributions to survey methodology, including the design, analysis, and quality of complex sample surveys, causes and corrections for nonresponse and measurement errors, and methods of combining multiple data sources.

TIMOTHY M. SMEEDING is the Lee Rainwater Distinguished Professor of Public Affairs and Economics at the La Follette School of Public Affairs at the University of Wisconsin-Madison. He was the founding director of the Luxembourg Income Study from 1983 to 2006 and was director of the Institute for Research on Poverty at UW Madison from 2008 to 2014. He is the 2017 John Kenneth Galbraith Fellow of the American Academy of Political and Social Science. Smeeding served on the board of directors of the National Academy on Aging and is an elected member of the National Academy of Social Insurance. He has served as head of the Economics of Aging Interest Group and is chair-elect of the Public Policy Committee for the Gerontology Society of America, where he was elected a fellow in 1990. Smeeding has written extensively on the topic of the economics of aging for numerous organizations and publications.

VETTA L. SANDERS THOMPSON *(Steering Committee Member)* is the E. Desmond Lee professor of racial and ethnic studies at the Brown School and associate dean for diversity, equity, and inclusion at Washington University in St. Louis. She also serves as co-director of the Center for Community Health Partnership and Research at the Institute for Public Health, is an associate member of the Siteman Cancer Center, a faculty affiliate of the Department of African and African-American Studies, and the Interdisciplinary Program in Urban Studies. She is a licensed psychologist and health service provider in the state of Missouri. Her research is focused on the health and well-being of ethnic and racial minorities, particularly the African American community. She is known for her work on racial identity, psychosocial implications of race and ethnicity in health behavior and determinants of health and mental health disparities. Sanders Thompson has conducted research on the promotion of cancer screening among African Americans and community engagement, including a Patient-Centered Outcomes Research Institute funded project to develop a measure of the quality of community and patient engaged research. Over the years she has been honored by the St. Louis community and by professional colleagues for efforts to improve service delivery in Black communities. She received her B.A. in psychology and social relations from Harvard University, and M.A. and Ph.D. in psychology from Duke University, where she also completed clinical training.

BETH VIRNIG is the director of the Research Data Assistance Center at the University of Minnesota. She is a trained epidemiologist with expertise in population-based measures of health and health care use, particularly in the use of administrative data such as those from Medicare, Medicaid, and All Payer Claims Database. Her research has used Medicare data alone and in combination with other data sources, including cancer registry data, data from local and federal surveys, and compiled geographical summaries, and she has examined access to health care and use and outcomes of that care, and how health care is influenced by patients, providers, and markets. Her research on the elderly in the Medicare program focuses on cancer surveillance and care, Medicare managed care, and end-of-life care.

LINDA WAITE is the George Herbert Mead Distinguished Service Professor of Sociology at the University of Chicago and Senior Fellow at NORC at the University of Chicago. She is principal investigator of the National Social Life, Health and Aging Project (NSHAP), widely recognized as the gold standard for the collection of survey data on older adults' intimate and social relationships and innovation in the development of methods for the collection of biomarkers such as blood spots and saliva during in-home interviews. As part of NSHAP's multidisciplinary investigatory team, Waite has participated in three rounds of data collection, with a fourth under way, a COVID-19 substudy, and numerous ancillary studies. Using unique data from NSHAP's partner dyads, Waite has expanded research and public discourse on later-life sexuality. Her widely published research demonstrates that sexuality is not just the province of the young. Waite has received numerous honors and awards for her scholarly contributions. Waite is also past president of the Population Association of America and was a member of the Advisory Board to the director of the National Institutes of Health (NIH). She has received a MERIT Award from NIH and is an elected member of the American Academy of Arts and Sciences.

NICOLE WATSON is a survey methodologist and associate professor at the Melbourne Institute within the University of Melbourne. She has worked on the Household, Income and Labour Dynamics in Australia (HILDA) Survey since 2000. Her role has covered many aspects of the HILDA Survey Project, including fieldwork contract management, weighting, and imputation.

DAVID WEIR is a research professor in the Survey Research Center at the Institute for Social Research at the University of Michigan and director of the Health and Retirement Study (HRS). He has led the transformation of the HRS into a world-leading biosocial survey combining its traditional excellence as a longitudinal economic survey with direct biological measures of health, genetics, linked medical and long-term care records from the Medicare system, and enriched psychological measurement. His research increasingly includes comparative analyses from the international family of HRS studies that now cover more than half the world's population, including the dementia assessments done with the Harmonized Cognitive Assessment Protocol developed by HRS for international comparisons. He received his Ph.D. in economics from Stanford University and previously held faculty positions at Yale and the University of Chicago.

COMMITTEE ON NATIONAL STATISTICS

The Committee on National Statistics was established in 1972 at the National Academies of Sciences, Engineering, and Medicine to improve the statistical methods and information on which public policy decisions are based. The committee carries out studies, workshops, and other activities to foster better measures and fuller understanding of the economy, the environment, public health, crime, education, immigration, poverty, welfare, and other public policy issues. It also evaluates ongoing statistical programs and tracks the statistical policy and coordinating activities of the federal government, serving a unique role at the intersection of statistics and public policy. The committee's work is supported by a consortium of federal agencies through a National Science Foundation grant, a National Agricultural Statistics Service cooperative agreement, and several individual contracts.